CHESTER IN 50 BUILDINGS

PAUL HURLEY

AMBERLEY

First published 2017

Amberley Publishing, The Hill, Stroud
Gloucestershire GL5 4EP

www.amberley-books.com

British Library Cataloguing in Publication Data.
A catalogue record for this book is available from the British Library.

ISBN 978 1 4456 7040 9 (print)
ISBN 978 1 4456 7041 6 (ebook)

Origination by Amberley Publishing.
Printed in Great Britain.

Contents

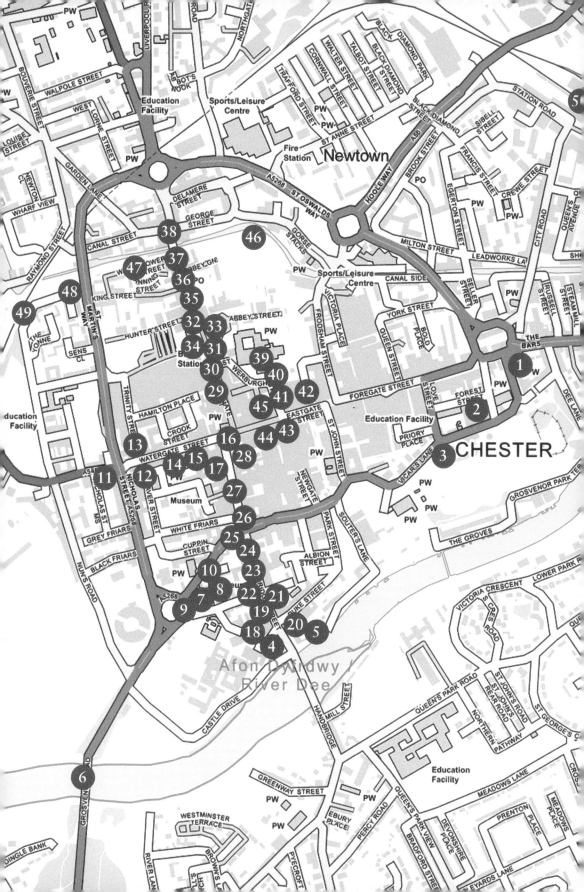

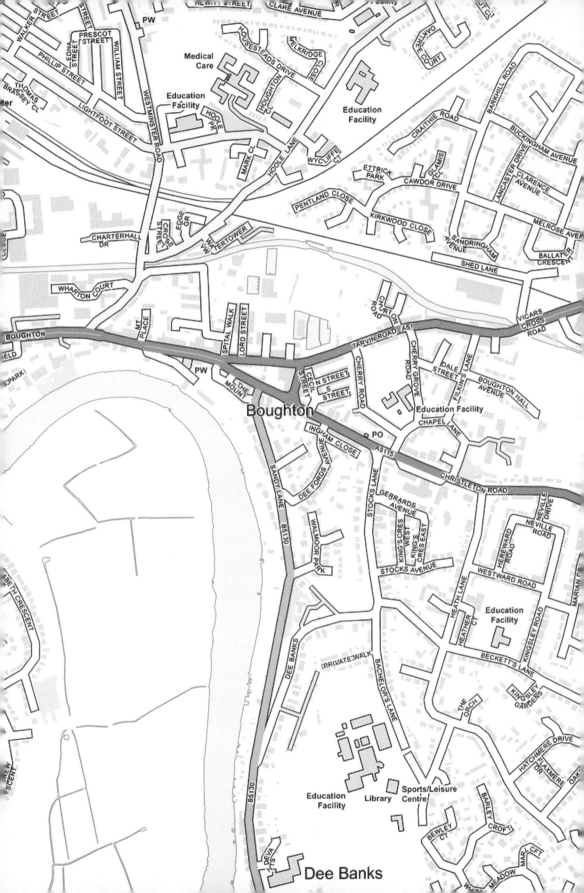

Key

1. Grosvenor Park Road
2. Chester City Baths
3. St John's Church
4. Bridgegate
5. Old Dee Bridge
6. Grosvenor Bridge
7. Chester Castle
8. Crown Court at the Castle
9. Gateway to Chester Castle
10. The Grosvenor Museum
11. Stanley Palace
12. Old Custom House Inn
13. The Old Custom House
14. Bishop Lloyd's Palace
15. God's Providence House
16. Chester High Cross
17. St Peter's Church
18. The Bear & Billet
19. Ye Old Edgar
20. St Olave's Church
21. Ye Olde Kings Head
22. Gamul House (now The Brewery Tap)
23. Oddfellows Hall
24. The Falcon
25. St Michael's Church
26. The Three Old Arches
27. The Dutch Houses
28. No. 1 Bridge Street
29. Commercial Coffee Rooms
30. Nos 3–31 Northgate Street
31. The Town Hall
32. The Coachworks
33. The Abbey Gateway
34. The Coach House
35. The Blue Bell
36. The Pied Bull
37. The Northgate and Gaol
38. The Bluecoat School
39. Chester Cathedral
40. The Music Hall Cinema
41. St Werburgh Street
42. Eastgate
43. The Grosvenor Hotel
44. Crypt Chambers
45. Ye Olde Boot Inn
46. The King Charles or Phoenix Tower
47. Morgan's Mount
48. The Goblin Tower
49. Bonewaldesthorne's Tower & Water Tower
50. Chester General Station

Introduction

During the Second World War many of Britain's cities were bombed to destruction. Coventry is the most notable example, but Liverpool, Birmingham, Plymouth and London, among many others, all saw their vistas change and their ancient buildings turned to rubble. The RAF bombed the ancient German cities of Lübeck and Rostock and a fuming German hierarchy instigated what were called the Baedeker Raids. These used the German Baedeker tourist guides that highlighted Britain's ancient towns and cities, and from these, militarily unimportant and picturesque towns, villages and beauty spots were targeted. Canterbury, Exeter, Bath, Norwich and York were subjected to these bombing raids. Chester somehow escaped the attentions of the Luftwaffe, perhaps because German planes were being lost for little military gain, and Field Marshal Erwin Rommel's fortunes had changed in the desert. Either way, the fortunes of war were turning in Chester's favour.

Whatever the reason, Chester was left almost bomb-free, even though it housed important war industries such as Vickers-Armstrong, which had its aircraft factory at Broughton. During the Second World War they built 5,786 Wellington bombers in the Broughton factory and, with a massive RAF airbase at nearby Sealand, there had to be some action. There was a succession of air raids in late 1940 and early 1941 but these achieved only slight damage. During the war there were 232 alerts: forty-four high-explosive bombs and three incendiaries were dropped on the city and, as a result, three people were killed and three seriously injured. While other cities were rebuilding from the rubble, Chester was left, fortunately, virtually unscathed, so picking fifty buildings from the plethora that exist in the cit of Chester was not an easy task (albeit many were lost during the building of the Inner Ring Road).

Chester is well known as a Roman city; it was called *Deva Victrix* around 2,000 years ago. After the Romans left the area towards the end of the fourth century it was left to rot for many years until the daughter of King Alfred of Wessex repaired, rebuilt and fortified it. Her title 'Aethelflaeda, Lady of the Mercians' was well deserved. As well as ruling Mercia, she led her troops into battle against the marauding Vikings. Around this time Chester became the county town, giving birth to the County Palatine of Chester. It is one of the jewels in Britain's crown and attracts tourists from around the world. The beautiful black-and-white buildings are mainly from the late nineteenth/early twentieth centuries and were designed by some of the best architects of their generation, one of whom, John Douglas, was described by architectural historian Nikolaus Pevsner as 'the very best Cheshire architect'.

This ancient walled city was once one of the most important Roman fortress towns in Great Britain. It stands astride the mighty River Dee, with its castle facing the Welsh border from whence, in days of yore, the invaders would come. Little of the original castle remains; it served the city and held back the Welsh hordes – well, most of them anyway! During the Civil War Chester's walls provided the viewing platform for the king's observation of one of the last major battles at Rowton Moor (or Rowton Heath) and these events on 24 September 1645 ended all hope of a Royalist victory.

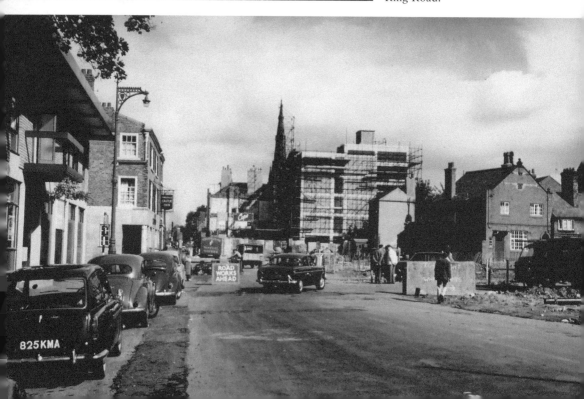

Left: Baedeker guidebook.

Below: Some of the destruction caused during the construction of the Inner Ring Road.

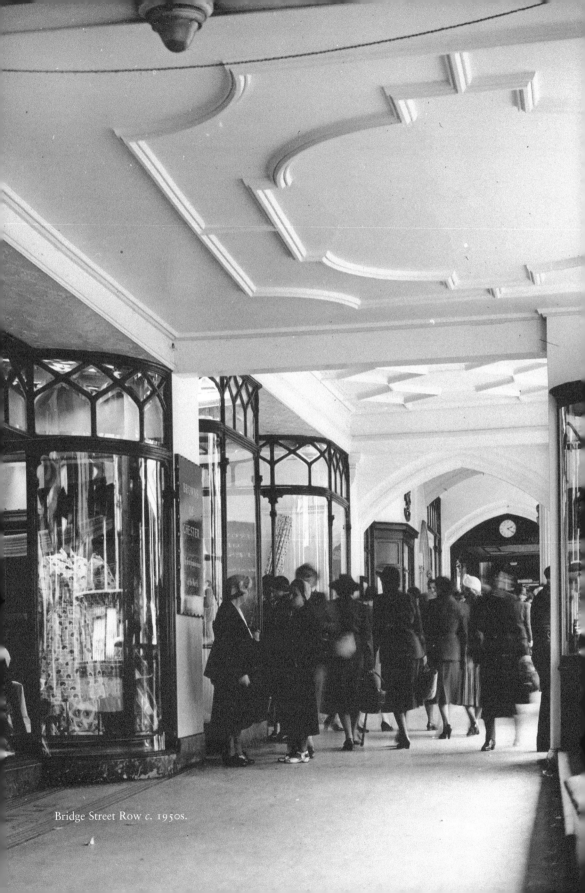

Bridge Street Row *c.* 1950s.

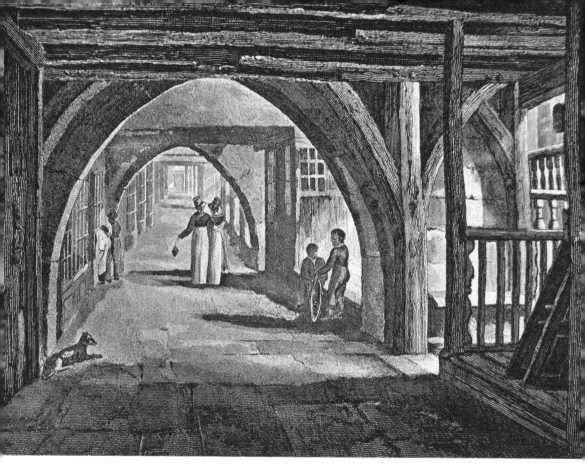

Chester's ancient Rows in Eastgate Street.

One of Chester's most famous historical features are the Rows. They are continuous half-timbered galleries which form a second row of shops above those at street level. They can be found along Eastgate Street, Northgate Street, Watergate Street and Upper Bridge Street. Nothing similar exists anywhere else in the world. They date from the medieval period and could originally have been designed to protect the pedestrian from the ordure and filth that would have been in the street at that time. It was also a convenient way of fitting more shops into a smaller footprint. Whatever the reason, they are certainly a feature to be enjoyed today.

In this book I have selected fifty buildings from the many impressive edifices that Chester boasts, but where do we start? Chester has the only complete perimeter wall in Great Britain, allowing the visitor to perambulate at their leisure completely around the city centre. I hope that you will enjoy this look into some of the most historically interesting buildings that Chester has to offer.

The 50 Buildings

1. Grosvenor Park Road

We start our tour in Grosvenor Park Road and are instantly faced with the most eccentric and beautiful of the buildings designed by Chester architect John Douglas. Nos 1–11 and No. 13 Grosvenor Park Road consists of a row of six attached cottages and a separate townhouse on the east side of Grosvenor Park Road. The cottages contain a touch of the Jacobean, Scottish Baronial, French, Spanish and Germanic, resulting in a truly eclectic and unusual row of houses. The National Heritage List for England (NHLE) has given them a Grade II listing. Nos 1–11 are constructed of buff red sandstone with tiled roofs of Westmoreland green slate, built in 1902 on land owned by John Douglas. Number 13 is a detached townhouse built in hard red brick. Douglas has designed beautiful buildings throughout Cheshire and Wales but here he has included bits of most of them. We see large plain gables with the upper storeys jettied on corbels, and three round turrets with conical roofs. Over the door to No. 11 is a plaque with the date 1903.

Another of John Douglas' triumphs are the houses in Port Sunlight Garden Village, built for Lever Brothers, and in Chester we see architectural elegance in a similar vein.

Grosvenor Park Road.

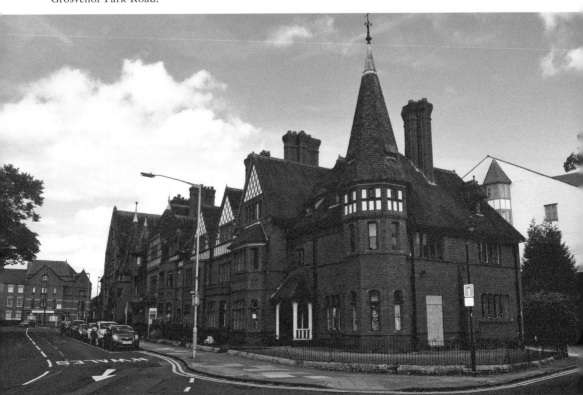

2. Chester City Baths

Chester City Baths at the junction of Bath Street and Union Street is another beautiful building, boasting architect John Douglas' trademark twisted chimneys. It can be found opposite Grosvenor Park that leads down to the River Dee. The Public Baths were built between 1898 and 1901 on land belonging to John Douglas. Because of the number of buildings designed and built by Douglas in this part of the city, it has been colloquially named 'Douglasville'.

Before these baths were built the locals had the option of some short-lived floating baths in the River Dee or at Bonewaldesthorne's Tower and the Water Tower off the City Walls. Neither were well-loved by the locals but this building and the swimming pool within it certainly were and they served the community well. The population continued to grow and a leisure centre and a modern swimming pool were needed. When Chester's Northgate railway station closed in 1969 and was subsequently demolished, the land was used to build the Northgate Arena containing the required leisure centre. The Bath Street Baths still stand and continue to serve the community today.

Chester City Baths.

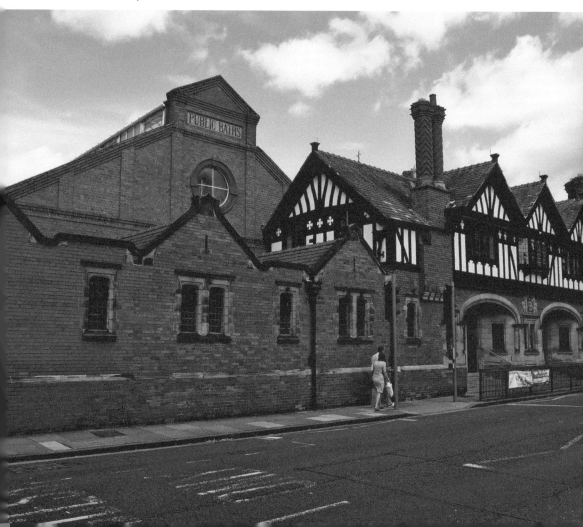

3. St John's Church

Continue along Union Street into Vicars Lane and we find the Church of St John the Baptist, once Chester Cathedral. This lane leads to Little St John Street, which curves around the north of the Amphitheatre site. Local historians pondered the location of the Amphitheatre, knowing that it was in Chester somewhere but having no idea where it was until a gardener from the Ursuline convent came across some stones during his gardening. He had found the Chester Roman Amphitheatre hidden completely for so long. Half of it has been brought back to life; the other half still lies beneath Dee House. A building now becoming derelict.

But back to St John the Baptist next to the Amphitheatre. In the late seventh century (AD 689) King Aethelred of Mercia founded the Minster Church of West Mercia on what is an early Christian site known as the Minster of St John the Baptist in Chester. It still stands today as St John the Baptist Church, which remains an open and active church and a Grade I-listed building. The church was for a while the Chester Cathedral; during the eleventh century Earl Leofric was a benefactor of the church, and in 1075 Peter, Bishop of Lichfield, moved his see to Chester, making St John's his cathedral until he died in 1085. His successor moved his seat to Coventry, and St John's became a co-cathedral.

It was a prominent place of worship undergoing continuous rebuilding until the Reformation and the Dissolution of the Monasteries, at which time it had much of the east end demolished. The ruins can be seen today. After the Dissolution, it became and remains a Church of England parish church. During the reign of Elizabeth I, the nave was restored and during the English Civil War it was used as a garrison by

St John's Church.

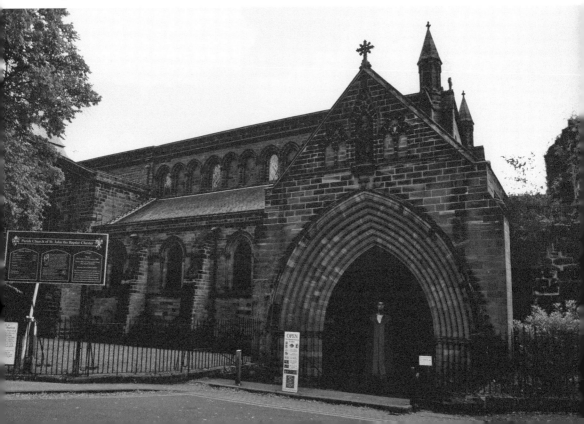

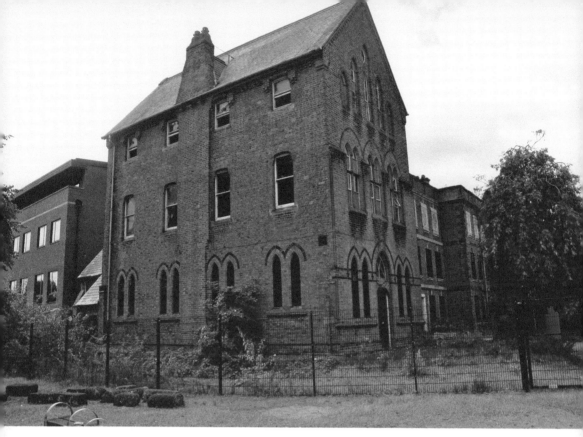

Above: Dee House.

Below: Interior of St John the Baptist Church.

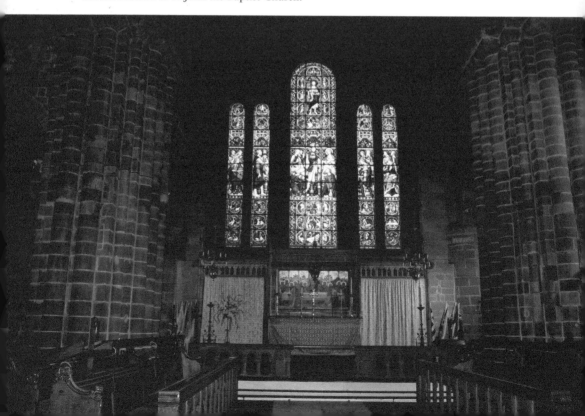

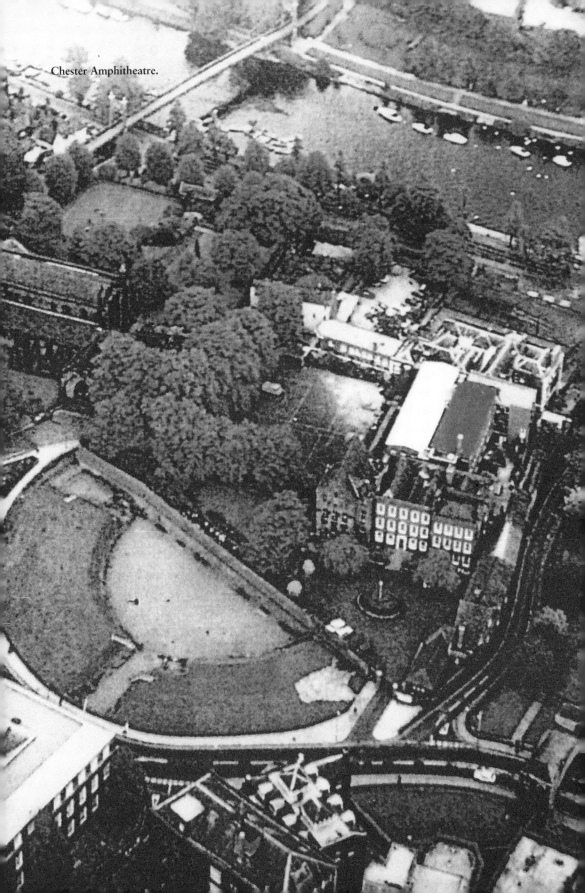

Chester Amphitheatre.

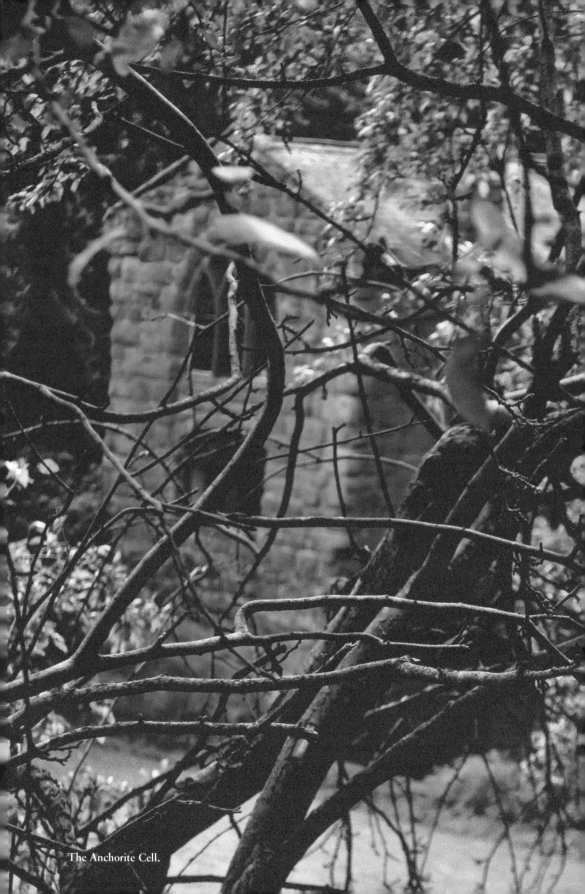

The Anchorite Cell.

Parliamentary forces. Building continued over the years as bits crumbled and were rebuilt. In the meantime, Henry VIII had turned the Monastery of St Werburgh into Chester Cathedral. A look inside St John the Baptist, however, offers the visitor a flavour of what was to be an impressive cathedral building had things been different.

In the church grounds overlooking the River Dee is an Anchorites Cell or hermitage, built to house a monk or nun as a hermit's religious retreat. Grade II listed, it has now been converted into a dwelling house. An Anchorite is a person who hides him- or herself away from the world to dedicate their life to God. It is reputed to be the hiding place of Harold the Saxon, King Harold, who supposedly died at the Battle of Hastings but in fact died a hermit in the Chester Anchorite Cell.

4. Bridgegate, Lower Bridge Street

Passing the Amphitheatre on the left, take the next left turn down Souter's Lane. Turn right at the bottom along The Groves until you come to the Bridgegate and the Dee Bridge. This gate allows access from Lower Bridge Street to the Old Dee Bridge, which was at one time the only crossing of the Dee into Wales. As such it was very heavily fortified to deter use by the Welsh during the many incursions onto English soil. During the twelfth century the Roman walls were extended and this section of the wall incorporated the original Bridgegate, which has been there since before the 1120s, as old records show that the sergeant of the gate had an office within the gateway.

Bridgegate, Lower Bridge Street, in 1900.

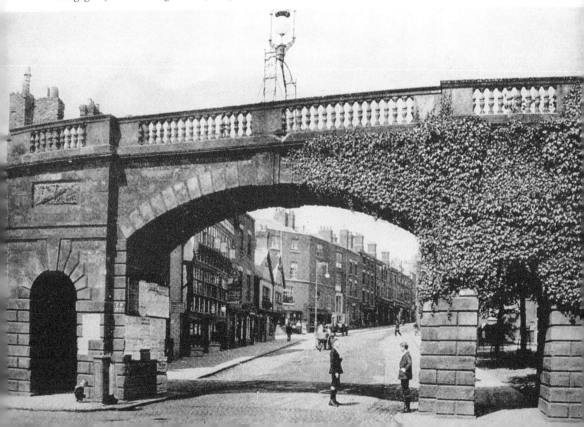

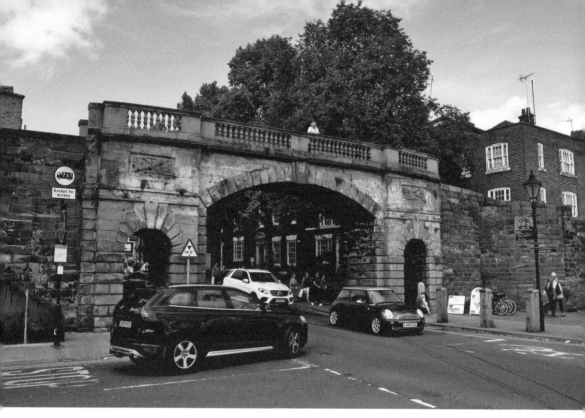

Bridgegate, Lower Bridge Street.

This gate guarded the southern entrance into the town and the road from Wales that crossed the bridge. It was rebuilt towards the end of the fourteenth century, at which time the gate would also have been rebuilt. In 1600 a square tower was added and this contained machinery for drawing water from the river for use in the city. The gate was destroyed in the Siege of Chester during the English Civil War and the present gateway and bridge were built in 1781, the architect being Joseph Turner.

5. Old Dee Bridge

This bridge across the River Dee to Handbridge was for many years the only route from Chester to North Wales, and until the building of the Grosvenor Bridge, it was the only crossing of the Dee into Wales. Hugh Lupus, the first Earl of Chester, ordered the building of the weir near the Dee Bridge in 1093; the weir is still there today and has a Grade I listing. Originally it drove the water towards the waterwheels of the Dee Mills near to the Bridgegate and the pumps that brought water into the city. In the year 911 there is record of a ferry at this location but the Old Dee Bridge was recorded in the Domesday Book in 1086, making it the oldest bridge in Chester. The early bridges were made of wood and were frequently washed away. In 1357 Edward the Black Prince (who was also the Earl of Chester in 1333 and Prince of Wales in 1343), ordered the Mayor of Chester to build it properly and provided his own mason and surveyor to assist.

That bridge is the one that we see today, albeit having been rebuilt and repaired over the years. It was the bridge that King Charles I used to escape the city after his troops were

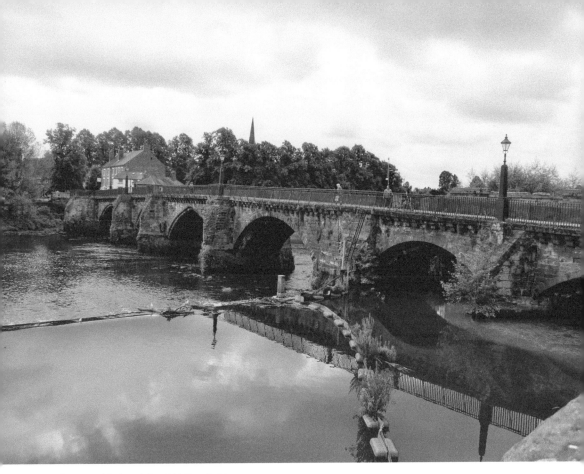

Above and below: The Old Dee Bridge.

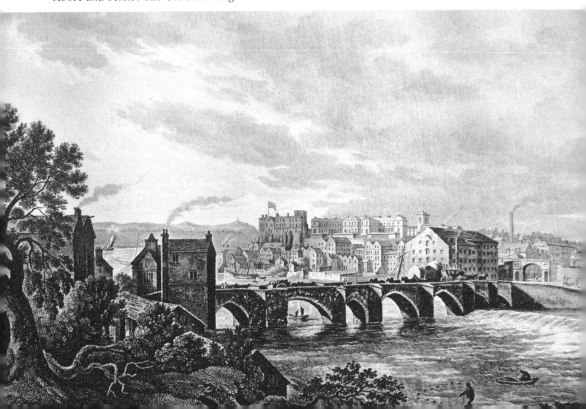

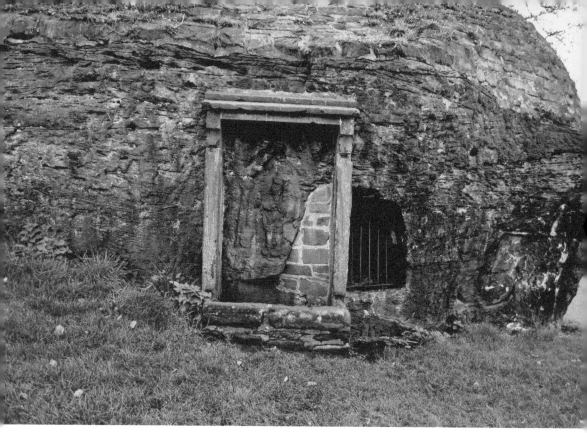

The statue of Minerva in Edgar's Field.

routed. In 1825–26 the bridge was widened by Thomas Harrison to provide the footway (Harrison went on to design the Grosvenor Bridge a few years later).

Not a building as such but well deserving of a mention as it is just on the other side of the Old Dee Bridge is the statue of Minerva, the Roman goddess of war. This Grade I-listed statue is the only monument of its kind in Western Europe that remains in its original position (although a cast of it can be found in the Grosvenor Museum). The carving has weathered over the centuries and suffered from some vandalism. Next to the shrine is an opening in the rock face known as Edgar's Cave. The shrine stands beside the route of the old Roman road that leads into the fortress of Deva from the south. It was the site of a quarry that provided some of the stone for the Chester Walls and other buildings.

6. Grosvenor Bridge

As we walk past the old County Hall/Town Hall/university building we come to the Little Roodee that is now a large pay and display car park. Walking up the hill to the main Grosvenor Road we pass a scale model of the Grosvenor Bridge set into the banking on the right. This model is listed and was built probably prior to the building of the bridge itself as a demonstration model. It was originally sited in Raymond Street but moved to this location during the 1980s.

The Grosvenor Bridge was at one time the longest single arch bridge in the world, and it is designated as a Grade I listed building. It is a single-span stone arch road bridge crossing

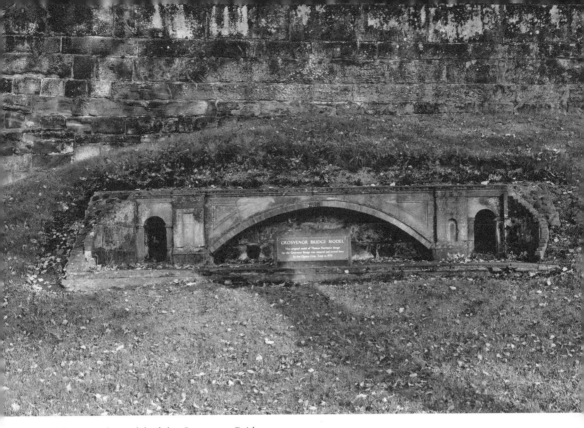

Above: Scale model of the Grosvenor Bridge.

Below: Grosvenor Bridge.

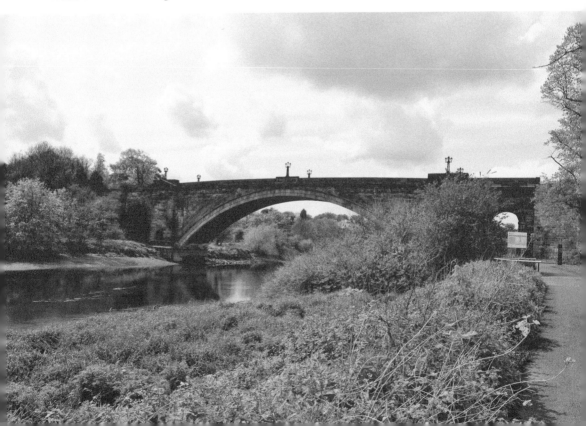

the River Dee and carries Grosvenor Road over the river. It was designed by Thomas Harrison and opened by Princess Victoria on 17 October 1832.

At the beginning of the nineteenth century, Chester only had one river crossing, the aforementioned Old Dee Bridge. Heavily congested, it delayed movement through the town. Building a new bridge over the Dee was prohibitively expensive until Thomas Telford proposed a new road between Shrewsbury and the Irish ferries at Holyhead to facilitate trade between the two islands. The route would have bypassed Chester, greatly reducing the potential income from the lucrative Irish trade routes. A committee was appointed to consider plans for a new bridge to quicken movement across the city and encourage traders to continue to stop there. Chester was at the time a major shipbuilding city, and a very tall bridge was required to allow ships to pass underneath. A design by the architect Thomas Harrison featuring bridge 60ft (18m) high and 200ft (61m) wide was chosen. Limestone was brought from Anglesey and this together with gritstone made up the building materials. The first stone was laid by the Marquess of Westminster on 1 October 1827. Construction was finally completed in November 1833, and a toll imposed to pay the £50,000 (around £4,020,000 today) construction costs, a hefty sum at the time.

The toll proved harmful to trade and was abolished in 1885, when maintenance was transferred to the Chester Corporation. Harrison died two years into construction; his pupil, William Cole, completed the job.

The bridge itself is shielded by foliage in the summer months but can be plainly seen in the winter.

7. Chester Castle

Continuing up towards Grosvenor Road, we see Chester Castle on the right. In 1069 William the Conqueror ordered the building of a castle on the site of an old Roman auxiliary fort that had stood there in AD 79. Chester was the last Saxon burgh to fall to William during his subjugation of Northern England. Hugh Lupus was the first Earl of Chester and he undertook the building of the castle. It was built in the form of a motte and bailey castle, the motte was a raised earthwork upon which the castle was built with an enclosed courtyard or bailey surrounded by a moat or ditch. Originally the castle was built with a wooden tower, but during the twelfth century this was replaced by a stone one, the Flag Tower, which is still there.

The Agricola Tower was originally the gatehouse to the castle until it was rebuilt. It has on the first floor the chapel of St Mary de Castro (St Mary of the Castle) where, in 1687, James II attended mass.

During the thirteenth century the walls of an outer bailey were built and the ditch around the Crown Court shows where this wall was, as it was once the encircling ditch. The wall itself was removed in the late eighteenth century to allow for the building of the County Court. Over the years many notable people were locked in the cellars of the Agricola Tower, including Richard II, the 1st Marquis of Montagu, and the wife of the Duke of Gloucester, to name but a few.

Both King Henry and King Edward used Chester Castle as a base for their incursions into Wales. They could carry and supply their troops by land or via the River Dee, as it was navigable from Chester all the way to the sea.

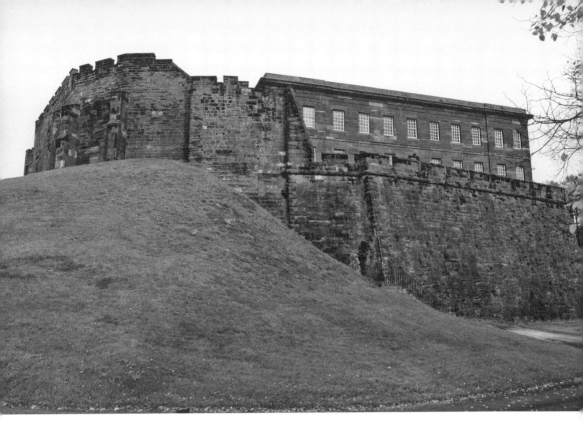

Above: Chester Castle and the old Town Hall.

Below: Chapel of St Mary De Castro.

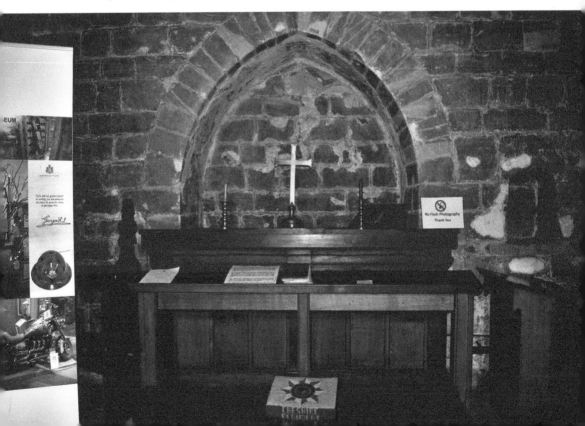

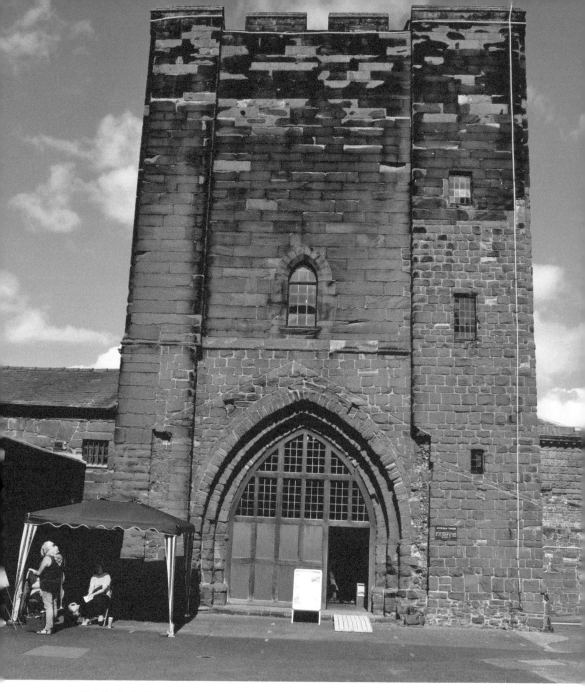

The Agricola Tower.

The County Gaol at this location was the main gaol for Chester and was built in 1798, although another existed at the Northgate. This gaol closed in 1808 and a new one, the City Gaol, was built in 1807, where the prisoners from both Chester and Cheshire county were executed. This lasted until 1871, when it too was closed and the prisoners moved to the ancient castle. In 1877 responsibility for prisoners was assumed by National Government and many gaols across the country were closed. Chester Castle gaol, however, continued

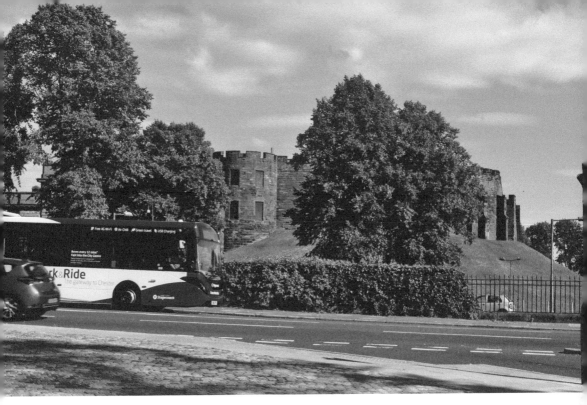

Chester Castle today.

as the county gaol, holding prisoners until 1884, when it ceased as a prison. The prisoners were moved to Knutsford gaol. This purpose-built prison and Sessions House had been built and opened in around 1820, when it assumed responsibility for the smaller prisons around the county, such as the one at Middlewich. In 1886 Chester gaol became a military prison and the scaffold was transferred to Knutsford. The main buildings of Chester gaol were demolished in 1900.

During the English Civil War Chester was held by the Royalists and it was aggressively assaulted during 1643 and 1645, when it was besieged. The castle suffered during the wars, both civil and with the Welsh, and the prison became unserviceable, so towards the end of the eighteenth century architect Thomas Harrison was commissioned to rebuild the prison and the castle. In 1873 the army moved into the castle and it became a depot for two battalions of the Cheshire Regiment. During 1925 the crypt of the Agricola Tower was reconsecrated as a chapel for the army residing in the castle. In 1939 the army moved to Dale Barracks.

8. Crown Court at the Castle

By the late 1700s the castle was in a poor state and a complete renovation was called for: Thomas Harrison was contracted for the job. Much demolition was carried out and the castle was fitted with a magnificent Shire Hall, Crown Courts, an armoury and Military Barracks. The work took place between 1788 and 1822. Fronting the castle was the Chester Crown Court. Through this spectacular gateway we find what is now the Crown Courts and Military Museum.

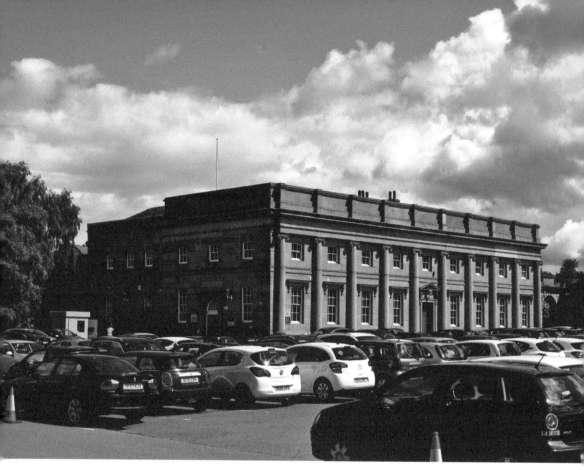

Above: Military Museum.

Below: Crown Court at the Castle.

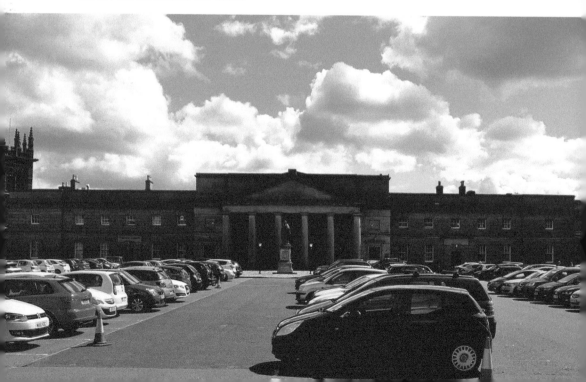

Harrison built two wings to the main building, one to act as barracks, now the Military Museum, and one to act as an armoury, later the Officer's Mess. The main Shire Hall became Chester Crown Court.

9. Gateway to Chester Castle

Harrison's pièce de résistance though was the gateway to Chester Castle. With its large stone columns and two lodges flanking the main gateway, it welcomed visitors from Wales and from within the city. It as massive portico-styled building in the form of a Propylaeum in Greek neoclassical style, with four widely spaced Doric columns. Historian Nikolaus Pevsner described it as 'one of the most powerful monuments of Greek Revival in the whole of England.'

The church tower in the background (when looking from the car park) was once St Mary's on the Hill; during the 1970s it closed as a church and became an educational centre. The statue in the road is of Field Marshal Stapleton-Cotton, 1st Viscount Combermere of Bhurtpore in the East Indies and of Combermere in Cheshire.

Crown Court and gateway.

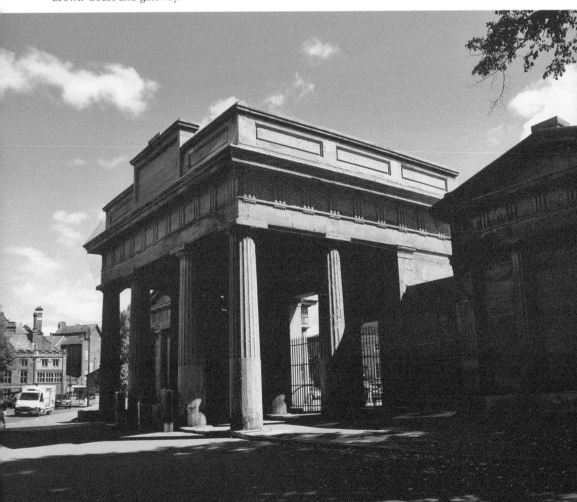

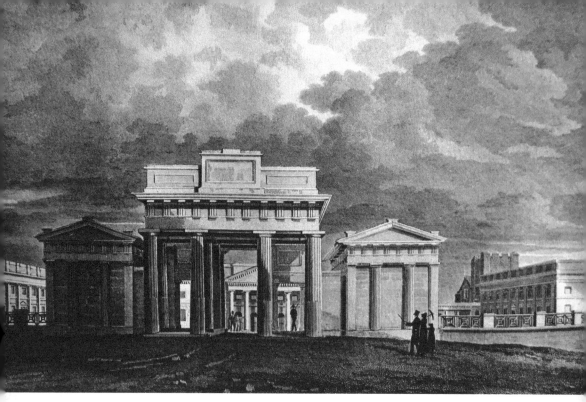

Ancient print of the gateway.

The people of Chester were so grateful for the work that Thomas Harrison had carried out in the city that they paid for a house for him. This is St Martins Lodge, which stands almost opposite the castle gateway. It was built as The Rectory and later became St Martins Villa; later still, when the police used it as offices, it was called St Martins Lodge. Today it is a very nice pub named – in honour of Harrison – The Architect.

10. The Grosvenor Museum

Passing into Grosvenor Street one of the first buildings we find is the Grosvenor Museum. Grosvenor was the family name of the Dukes of Westminster, whose home is in Chester and whose family have supported the city over the years. The name Grosvenor can be found on many establishments, including the Grosvenor Hotel. Hugh Richard Louis Grosvenor is the current 7th Duke, inheriting the title from his father, who died suddenly in 2016. The family seat is at Eaton Hall.

Housed in a beautiful Grade II-listed red-brick building, the Grosvenor Museum was founded in 1885. The plot of land on Grosvenor Street was given to the founders by the 1st Duke of Westminster, who also donated £4,000 (£320,000 in today's money). Thomas Lockwood was appointed as the architect and the foundation stone was laid in 1885 by the 1st Duke (the museum was opened by him a year later). A major extension was built in 1894 and in 1915 the City of Chester took over the administration of the museum. In 1938 the authority took full control of the collections and displays. Today, Chester has a first-class museum and, just a few hundred yards away, the excellent Cheshire Military Museum in the grounds of the Crown Court and Chester Castle.

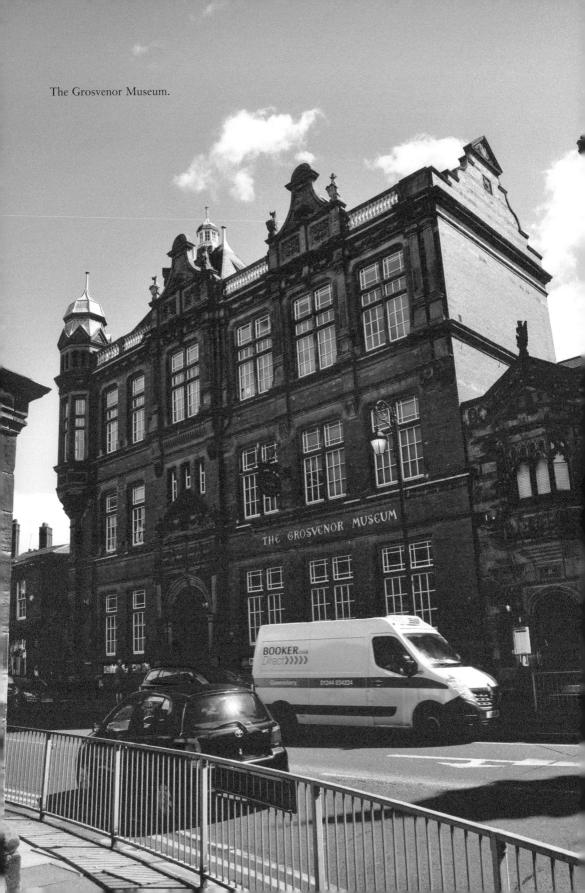

The Grosvenor Museum.

11. Stanley Palace

Crossing the road past the Magistrates' Court we come to Nicholas Road, which is in fact part of the Chester Inner Ring Road, and on our left we see an impressive row of Georgian terraced houses. These were designed by Joseph Turner and built in 1780, originally consisting of ten townhouses. Because many of the houses were used as doctor's surgeries, the row became known as 'Pillbox Promenade'. It is the longest and most uniform of the Georgian properties in Chester. Before the Inner Ring Road was built, Nicholas Road was a narrow road leading out of the city.

When we reach the crossroads of Nicholas Road and Watergate Street we find the beautiful black-and-white façade of Stanley Palace, said to be the most haunted building in Chester. It was built in 1591 on the site of a former Black (Dominican) Friary as a townhouse for Sir Peter Warburton. Sir Peter was a Chester solicitor and Member of Parliament. When he died in 1621 his daughter Elizabeth inherited the house and she married Sir Thomas Stanley of Alderley, who gave the house its name. He was High Sherriff of Cheshire and during the Civil War he supported the Parliamentarian cause, but towards the end of the Protectorate gave support to Charles II and was given a baronetcy when the Crown was restored.

Stanley Palace.

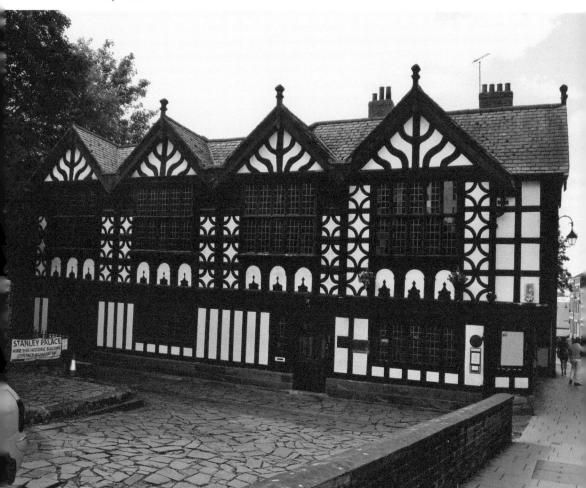

On the death of Sir Thomas, Elizabeth married into the Grosvenor family of Eaton Hall, and Stanley Palace went through years of neglect and rebuilding. By the end of the nineteenth century the house was no longer a palace but had been split into a number of cottages and apartments. In 1865 it was bought by the Chester Archaeological Society, known then as the Chester and North Wales Archaeological, Architectural and Historic Society' in 1866, partly it is rumoured to stop it being transported to America! After that it spent time as a boys' school. In 1889 it was sold to the 15th Earl of Derby and became a museum, known as Derby House. In 1911, during restoration works, tunnels were discovered leading to Chester Castle and the Watergate. In 1928 the building was donated to Chester City Council. Today it is under the stewardship of the Trustees of the Friends of Stanley Palace, a registered charity, and is available to hire.

12. The Old Custom House Inn

This building, now The Old Custom House Inn, was built originally as two adjoining houses, No. 69 which dates from 1637 and No. 71 which dates from the 1700s. In 1637 No. 69 was built for Thomas and Anne Weaver. The lane at the side is called Weaver Street after them and you can still see their initials – T & A W – carved on the building. Part of Chester's Rows formerly passed through the buildings, but this was enclosed in 1711. When it opened as a pub it was called the Star Inn, but later changed its name in the

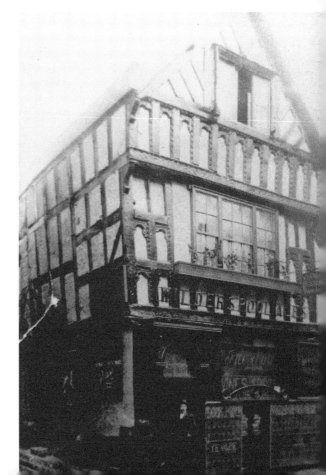

Old Custom House Inn, 1905.

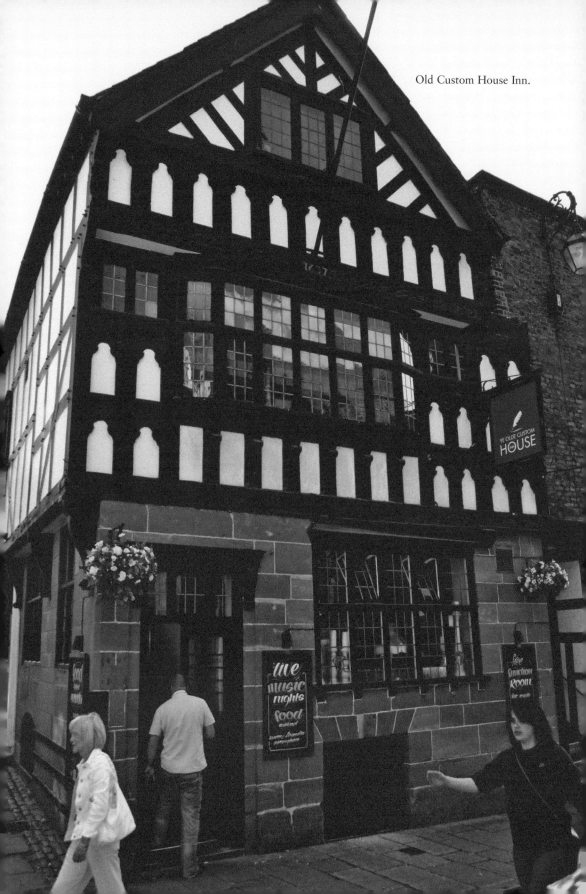

Old Custom House Inn.

eighteenth century to reflect the Custom House of the port of Chester, which stood across the road. The houses' undercrofts now form part of the inn's cellars. In 1828 the landlord was J. Walker. In the 1950s, when Wales was 'dry' on a Sunday, this was the only pub in Chester selling Border Ales from Wrexham. On a Sunday night it was packed! The building is now Grade II listed and like all such dated buildings it has been altered over the years, the latest being in 1990, when it was extended to the rear.

13. The Old Custom House

In the days when Chester was a thriving port, goods were brought ashore from ships arriving from all four corners of the world. They would be brought up Watergate Street from the Watergate to the Custom House. Here dues would be paid prior to onward sale in the city centre and elsewhere. From the Middle Ages to Tudor times the Comptroller of Chester Port was responsible and senior to the ports, from Barmouth in mid-Wales as far as the Scottish Borders, including the port of Liverpool. The offices for most of this time were situated within the Chester Castle precincts until 1633.

The old Custom House is situated at No. 70 Watergate Street. It was thought to have been built in 1633 when the customs offices were transferred from Chester Castle. The building

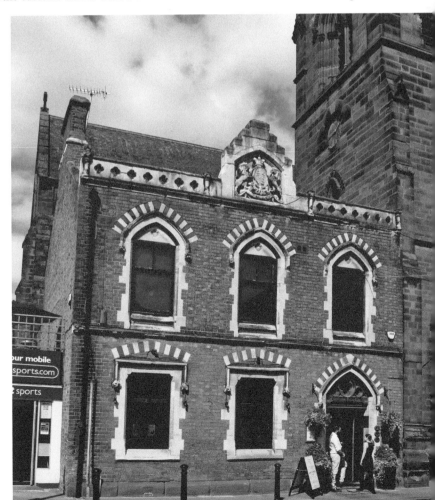

The old Custom House.

was rebuilt in 1868 to a design by James Harrison (who died at the age of fifty-two in 1866); the church next door was rebuilt at the same time, again to Harrison's design. By the beginning of the 1800s Chester's importance as a dock had vastly diminished, although the Custom House continued to support a staff of seven almost to the end of the century.

Watergate Street ran from the Watergate to the Chester Cross on the junction of Upper Watergate Street. On the corner is the building that used to be Holy Trinity Church. The original church that occupied this site probably dated from the fourteenth century, perhaps serving the seamen from the port below. The present church was built between 1865 and 1866 to a design by James Harrison, who died before the building was completed. The church closed in 1960 and since then has been Chester's Guildhall.

14. Bishop Lloyd's Palace

Continuing along Upper Watergate Street, we arrive at No. 41 Watergate Street, No. 51/53 Watergate Row, and a building known as Bishop Lloyd's Palace (or House). This ancient house originated as two houses which were built on medieval undercrofts and then rebuilt during the seventeenth century, when the two buildings were converted into one. The house has been associated with George Lloyd (1561–1615), who was Bishop of Sodor and Man and subsequently Bishop of Chester from 1605 until his death in 1615. He is buried in Chester Cathedral. This probably accounts for the seventeenth-century carving on the front elevation, which includes the Legs of Man and three horse's heads for both the bishopric

Fiesta Havana in the undercroft of Bishop Lloyd's Palace.

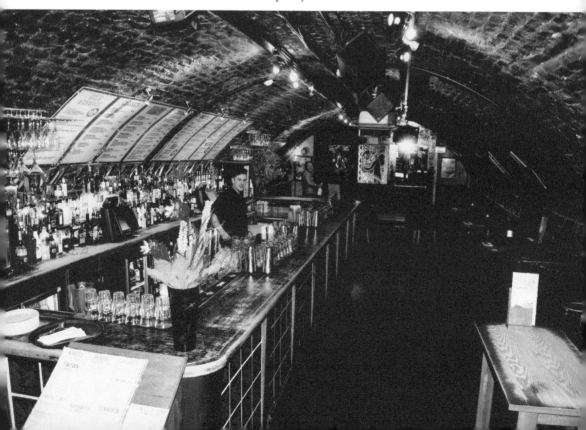

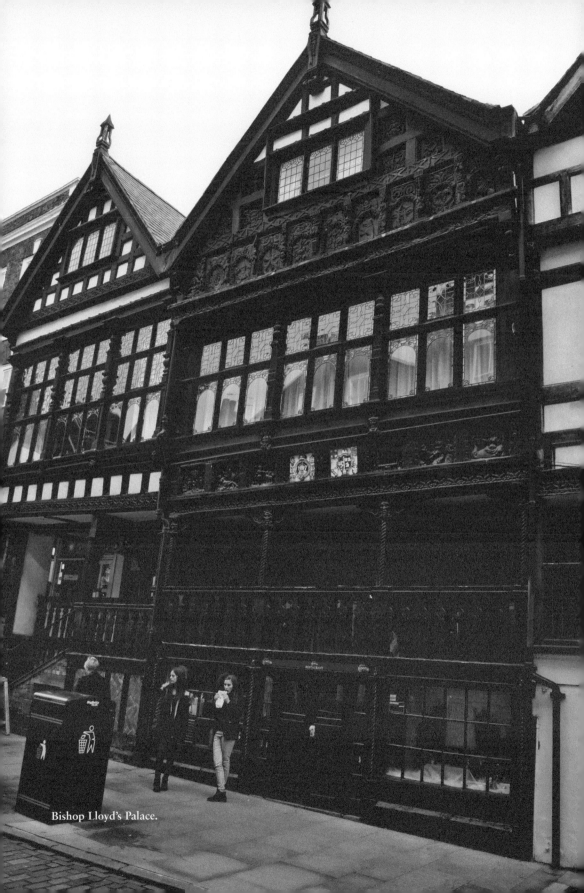

Bishop Lloyd's Palace.

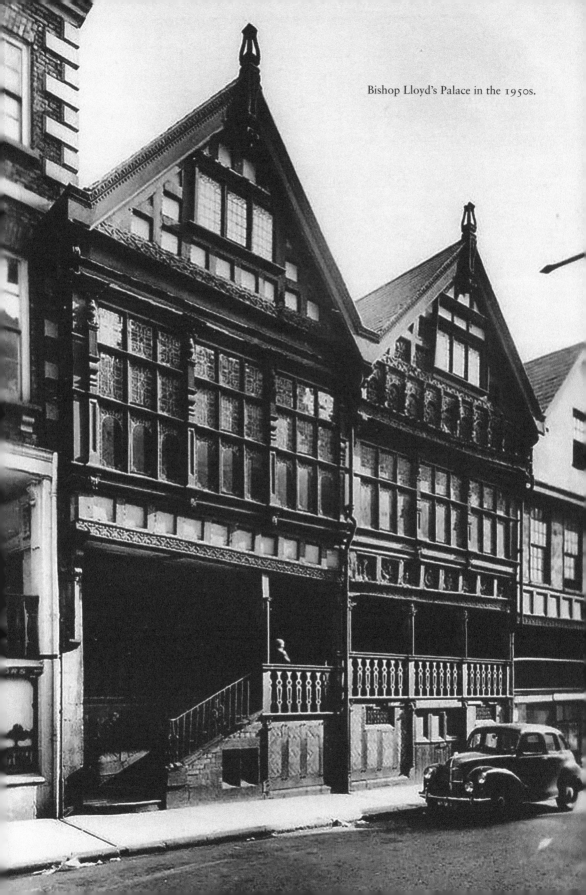

Bishop Lloyd's Palace in the 1950s.

and the Lloyd family. Interestingly, the Stanley family (of Stanley Palace) were very involved in the Isle of Man, as were the Earls of Derby.

By the nineteenth century the house had become rundown, the carvings on its frontage had been covered with plaster and the house split into tenements. In the 1890s the house was heavily restored by Thomas Lockwood, and a further restoration was carried out between 1973 and 1977. Pevsner described it as 'perhaps the best house in Chester' and today it is Grade I listed. The building now houses the Chester Civic Trust and is available for visits and for hire subject to the Trust's permission.

Today, in one of the old undercrofts, is the Fiesta Havana tapas bar, which is well worth a visit if only to view the ancient architecture.

15. God's Providence House

Continuing along Upper Watergate Street we come to another example of the work of James Harrison. It is an appropriate time perhaps to differentiate between the two architects called Harrison. Thomas Harrison (1744–1829) was born in Yorkshire and buried at Chester; he designed the Grosvenor Bridge and the prison. James Harrison (1844–66) was born and buried in Chester; he tended to specialise in churches and is

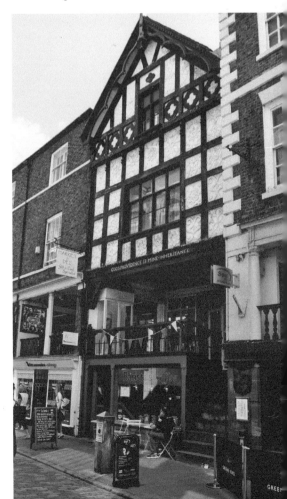

God's Providence House.

the pioneer of Black-and-White Revival in building architecture. This particular building is better known as God's Providence House and is one of James Harrison's exceptions. Number 9 Watergate Street, which includes Nos 11 and 11A Watergate Row, is a Grade II-listed building. To prevent this notable building from being demolished came Chester and North Wales Archaeological, Architectural and Historic Society to the rescue, who successfully campaigned for it to remain safe and be restored.

The building originally on this site dated from the thirteenth century and the present house was built in 1652, incorporating some timbers from the original building. The name of the house comes from one of Chester's plague visitations when, during an outbreak in 1647/48 which killed 2,000 people in the city, the people in the building on this site were spared the disease. This house was not built until about four years after that plague, so the name probably carried forward from the previous building on the site.

16. The Chester High Cross

At the end of Upper Watergate Street we find Chester's most famous antiquity, the Chester High Cross. The High Cross is situated at the junction of Northgate Street, Eastgate Street, Watergate Street and Bridge Street. The centre of the city for hundreds of years, it was also the location of the Roman Principia, where the Church of St Peter is now. The roads were set by the Romans, with each road leading away from the High Cross in the city centre. The area is now known colloquially as 'The Cross'. This medieval cross was destroyed during the Civil War in the name of iconoclasm, when religious artefacts were summarily

The Chester High Cross.

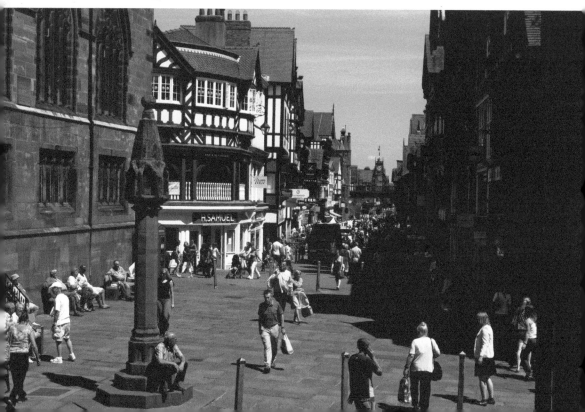

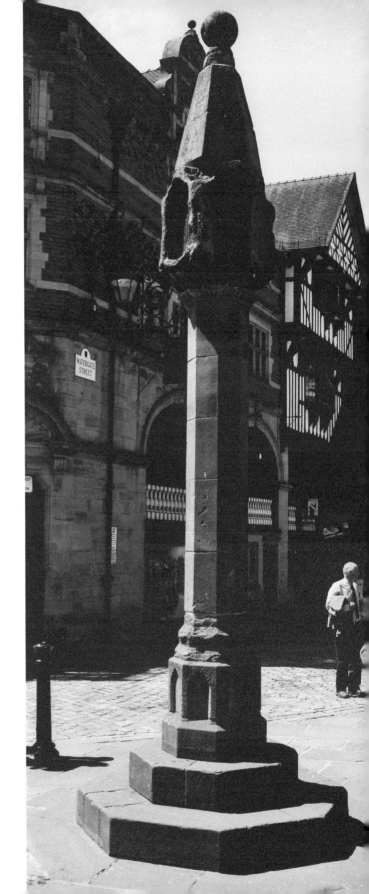

The Chester High Cross.

smashed and carried off. In the case of the Chester High Cross, this was for use elsewhere, for instance under the steps in the church, while the base was taken to Plas Newydd, the home of the 'Ladies of Llangollen' in Wales, where it still lies. The only truly original piece is the top of the shaft, which once contained small statues in the niches. It was not until 1804 that some pieces of the cross were recovered from beneath the church steps and given to Sir John Cotgreave for use in the garden of his new house, Netherleigh at Handbridge, but eventually they were returned to the city – the head of the cross going to the Grosvenor Museum. Later, the High Cross, with new additions, was re-erected elsewhere but returned to the city in the 1970s from whence it came. This area has always been of immense importance to Chester and it was here in 1649 that Charles I was declared a traitor. It was a place where felons were pilloried, bulls were baited and other sports of the period were carried out for the delectation of the people of Chester. Today, Chester's Town Crier declares from the High Cross.

17. St Peter's Church

Situated beside the Chester High Cross is this ancient church. The parish church, dedicated to St Peter, was founded in AD 907 by the Lady Æthelfleda and some of its fabric dates from that time. The church stands on the site of part of the former Roman Praetorium and was in 1086 referred to as 'Templum Sancti Petri' in the Domesday Book. The present church

St Peter's Church.

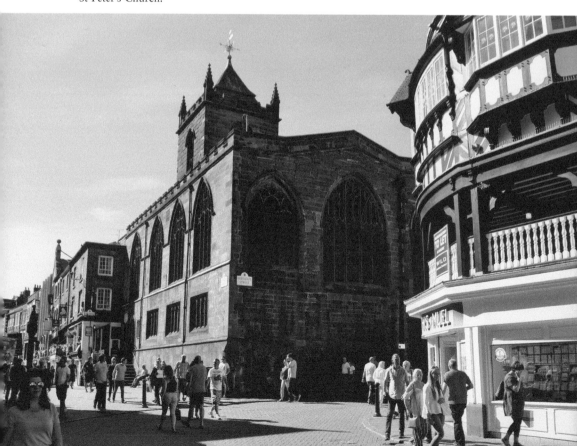

dates from the fourteenth, fifteenth and sixteenth centuries, with further modifications in the following three centuries. Formerly the tower had a spire which was removed and rebuilt in the sixteenth century, taken down in the seventeenth century, then rebuilt and finally removed, 'having been much injured by lightning', in around 1780. In 1849–50 the church was repaired by James Harrison and in 1886 it was restored by John Douglas, which included the addition of a pyramidal spire.

The St Peter's Church now looks serenely down Upper Bridge Street and is a Grade I-listed building. Note the church clock: there has been a clock on the tower since 1579 – when one was purchased for the sum of 2/6d – and it had to be regularly wound. It was only in 1973 that the need to wind it by hand ceased and electricity took over. Behind the church today is St Peter's churchyard, which can be accessed via The Victoria public house and a path in Northgate Street to the rear.

18. The Bear & Billet

A walk now down to the bottom of Bridge Street and the Watergate, where we find the ancient black-and-white-timbered Bear & Billet, one of Chester's best-known public houses. It was built in 1664 and this date is prominently shown on the front elevation. Prior to this there was an ancient building on the site that was destroyed during the English Civil War. It is one of the last wooden buildings built in the city and it was built

The Bear & Billet in Lower Bridge Street.

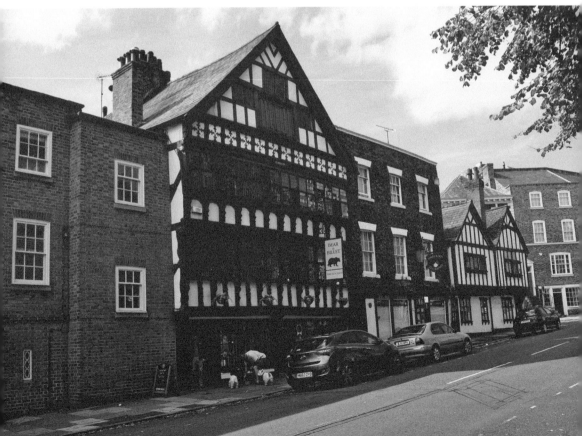

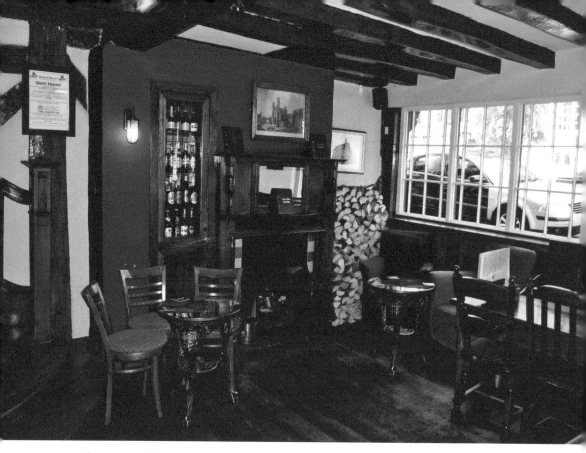

The Bear & Billet interior.

as the townhouse for the Earl of Shrewsbury, who was at the time one of the Serjeants of the Bridgegate. This entitled him to collect tolls from people passing through the nearby gate. It has been a pub since the eighteenth century and was at one time known as The Bridgegate Tavern. Due to its proximity to the Dee Mills there is evidence to show that it may also have been a grain warehouse – in the gable end there is a hoist above a set of double doors.

In 1820 General Grosvenor was thrown from the Dee Bridge into the river by his political opponents as he was crossing in his carriage; he was offered help and safety at the pub. It is recorded as a Grade I-listed building and has been described as 'the finest 17th century timber framed town house in Chester and one of the last of the great timber-framed town houses in England.' Its name could be taken from the heraldic device on the coat of arms of the Earl of Warwick, which consists of a bear tied to a billet or stake. However, according to the *Dictionary of Pub Names*, the Chester Bear & Billet refers not to any heraldic symbol but to a billet used in its older sense, as a thick piece of wood used as a weapon.

John Lennon's maternal grandmother, Annie Jane Milward, was born at the pub in 1873 and lived there until she was in her 20s. The Bear & Billet was refurbished in 1999 and renamed Bensons at the Billet in 2000. However, the locals were not happy about this and a year later it reverted to the Bear & Billet, and continues today to serve under its ancient name. Walking through the door is like stepping back in time: all dark wood, old-fashioned glass windows and the ambience of another era.

19. Ye Old Edgar

Continuing up Bridge Street we come to the former Ye Olde Edgar inn, situated at nos 86 and 88 Lower Bridge Street on the junction with Shipgate Street. This ancient building, now Grade II listed, was two houses when it was built in the sixteenth century and was later combined to become an inn. For many years thereafter it was the Ye Olde Edgar, later becoming the King Edgar and The Edgar Tavern. The name comes from King Edgar, who became the King of all England in 959. In 973 Edgar marched his army to Chester. This was in the days when Chester had a port and his navy met him in Chester via the Irish Sea. This show of strength persuaded the Northern kings to submit to him as their king. It is then reputed that he was rowed up the Dee to St John the Baptist Church by Kings Kenneth of Alba, Malcolm of the Cumbrians, Magnus of Man & the Isles, Donald of Strathclyde, Lago of Gwynedd and Princes Hywel of Gwynedd, Ithel and Sifert. As well as the pub name, Edgar's Field is a park in Chester. As for Ye Olde Edgar, after the inn closed it became derelict. It has now been restored and is once again two private houses.

Ye Old Edgar – now two private houses.

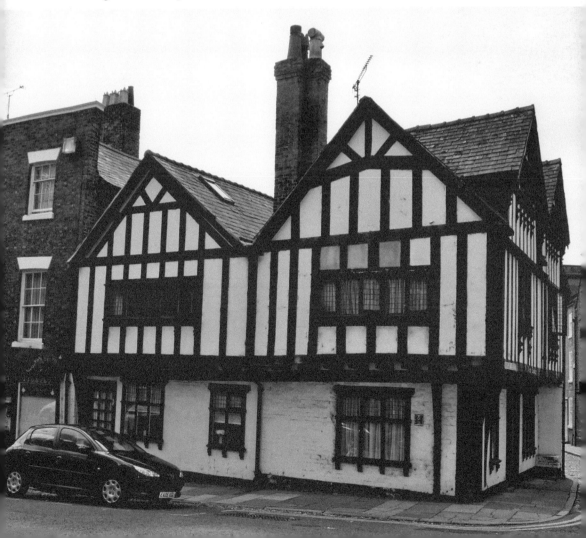

20. St Olave's Church

Continuing up Bridge Street we reach Ye Olde Kings Head. Over the road we have the ancient Church of St Olave's, situated in Lower Bridge Street. This is an area that was in the very early days a Scandinavian/Viking settlement, probably due to its location near to the port of Chester. The church is one of the oldest buildings in the city; the parish was founded in the eleventh century and is dedicated to Ólaf Haraldsson, a Norwegian king martyred in 1030. The reason for Ólaf's sainthood was, a year after he had died and been interred, his coffin was opened to find that his hair had grown and his cheeks were rosy!

The present church dates from 1611. In 1841 the parish was united with St Michael's at the Pepper Street/Bridge Street junction, now the Chester Heritage Centre. James Harrison restored the building and converted it for use as a school. In 1972 it was declared redundant and has since been used as a Pentecostal church and exhibition centre. At the time of writing it is supported by scaffolding and wooden planks.

Of interest, there are fifty-seven churches in Britain named in honour of St Olave.

St Olave's Church.

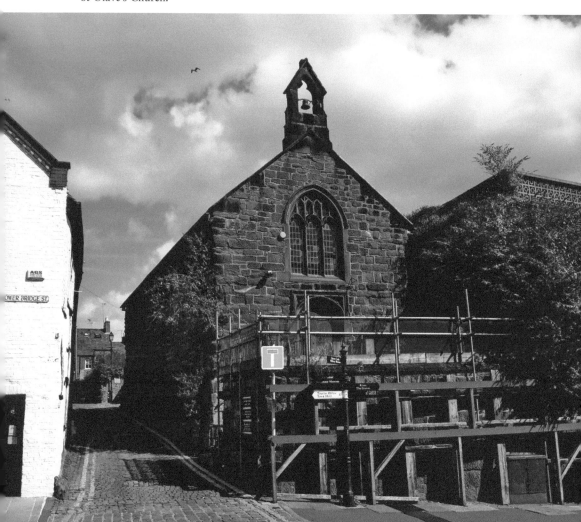

21. Ye Olde Kings Head

Crossing the road we find another beautiful black-and-white-timbered public house, Ye Olde Kings Head Hotel at Nos 48–50 Lower Bridge Street. This is on the junction of Lower Bridge Street and Castle Street, which leads up to the castle. It was constructed in 1622 for Peter Clerk, the administrator of Chester Castle. The foundations date back to 1208 and the front elevation can be dated back to the seventeenth century. It first became a pub in 1717. It once contained a section of the Rows but these were closed during the early eighteenth century.

The latest of these alterations were made for Randle Holme, the Chester historian and first mayor of Chester (from 1633 to 1634) and was described at the time as a 'new building'. The building was restored in 1935 and again in the 1960s. The pub still boasts an Elizabethan fireplace. On the side wall in Castle Street is a rather unique iron plaque that warns people to 'Commit no Nuisance'.

This pub is supposedly one of the most haunted buildings in Chester. On display in the bar is a framed sword and slippers that were discovered under the floorboards in one of the rooms dating from the seventeenth century.

Ye Olde Kings Head in Victorian days.

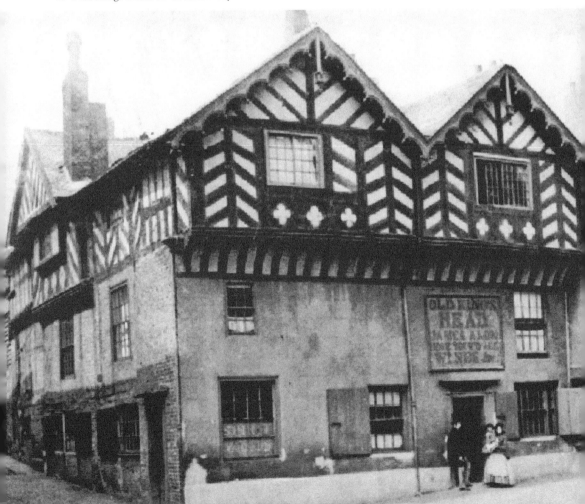

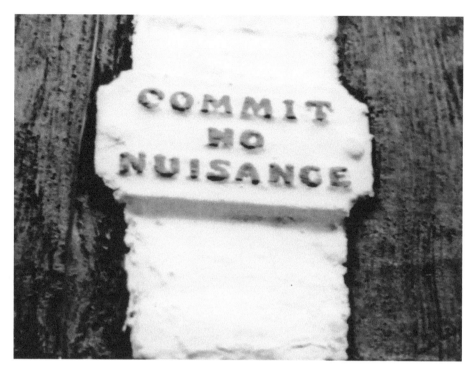

Above: Wall sign at Ye Olde Kings Head.

Below: Ye Olde Kings Head.

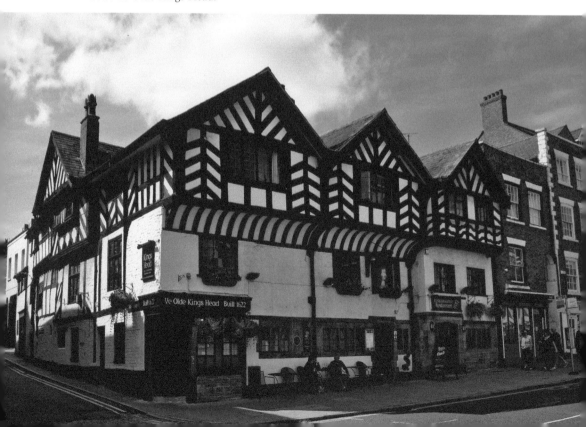

22. Gamul House (now The Brewery Tap)

Continuing up Lower Bridge Street we come to a popular pub called The Brewery Tap, a new pub in an ancient building at nos 52–58. Set back from the road and up a short stairway, this building stretches way back in Chester's history. Known as Gamul House, the building was once a Jacobean Great Hall built for the Gamul family and is the only stone-built medieval hall to survive in Chester. The Gamul family were wealthy merchants in the city and powerful enough to support their own army. This army was lent to King Charles I, who stayed here from 23–26 September 1645.

Parts of the present Gamul Hall date from around the early sixteenth century, with the oldest visible areas being the wall and fireplace behind the bar. In those early days, most buildings were built from wood with manure and mud infills. After such fires as the Great Fire of London, local councils stared to look at these wooden structures and the medieval façade of Gamul House was changed for a brick-built one, not quite as attractive perhaps, but a lot safer. At the top of the steps can be found the only bit of the Rows in Lower Bridge Street. The street lost most of its Rows after the Civil War, and the owners of the present Falcon pub did not help in applying successfully to incorporate their Row into the building (an incentive taken up by other owners in the street). Fortunately, The Brewery Tap still retains a bit of the Rows.

The Gamul family lived here during the sixteenth and seventeenth centuries. Thomas Gamul was the city's recorder and his father was mayor on four occasions. His son, Sir Francis, was a staunch Royalist and resided here during the Civil War. He was responsible for the city's defences and the last time that Charles I stayed was the night before the Battle of Rowton Moor (or Rowton Heath), and it was from here that he made the short walk with Sir Francis to the walls of Chester to watch his army lose decisively to the Parliamentarians. (The king later made his escape across the Old Dee Bridge and into Wales; he was imprisoned

Ancient painting of the Gamul House.

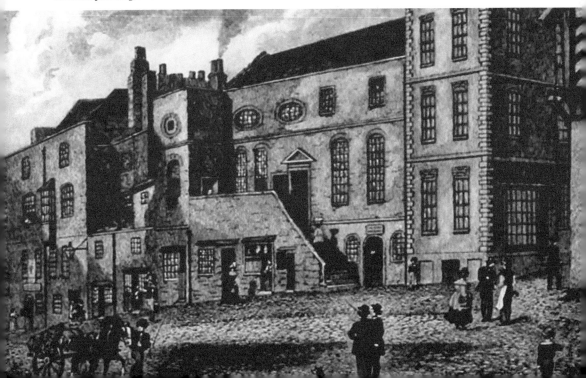

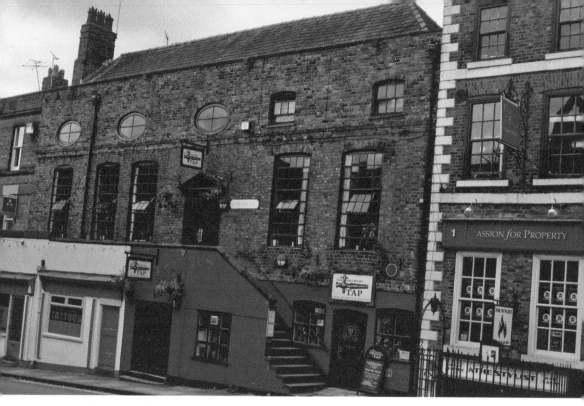

Above: Gamul House, now The Brewery Tap.

Below: Modern interior of the Great Hall.

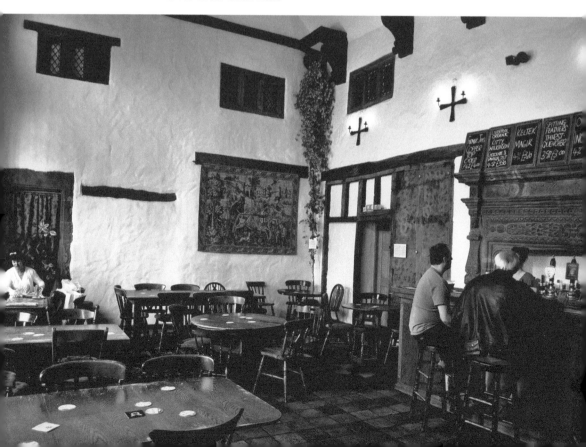

and executed in January 1649.) Chester was badly damaged during the siege that followed and this was acerbated by the onset of the plague that killed nearly 2,000 people. Being on the losing side, Sir Francis had his lands seized by Parliament. The family tomb is at St Michael's Church at the top of the road, now Chester's Heritage Centre.

Over the years Gamul House became rundown and when historian Nikolaus Pevsner inspected it in the 1960s he reported that it looked derelict. Chester City Council then bought it and in the 1970s started a full refurbishment. On the fireplace behind the bar is a painting of the arms of the Gamul family. Pevsner identified this as being executed by the historian and heraldic artist Randle Holme.

On 20 November 2008 it was opened as The Brewery Tap, selling locally brewed ale from the Spitting Feathers brewery. This brewery is located at Waverton on the outskirts of Chester, which just happens to be near the famous battlefield of Rowton Moor!

23. Oddfellows Hall

As we continue up Lower Bridge Street we come to a large and impressive Grade II-listed building that is now an attractive boutique hotel and bar. It was built in 1676 for Lady Mary Calverley and was originally called Bridge House, a large neoclassical town house. She petitioned the City Assembly for permission to demolish the original house (which contained a section of the Chester Rows) and replace it with a new house. This was granted and during the rebuilding, like The Falcon further up Lower Bridge Street, the Rows were incorporated into

Oddfellows Hall.

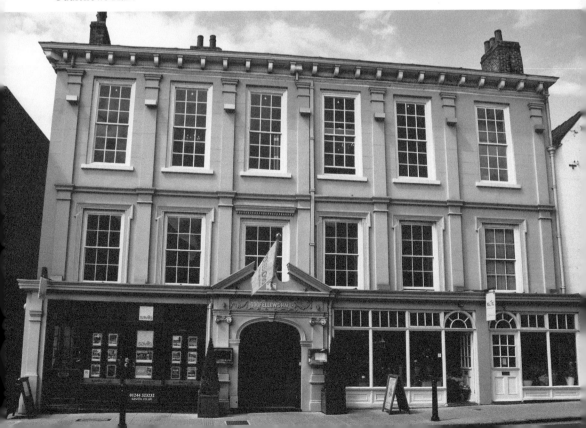

the building. It was also the first building to be built in Chester city centre in a classical style. Lady Mary was fined £20 for the illegal act of doing away with the Rows (this would be around £3,000 today). During the eighteenth century the house was occupied by the local Attorney General, John Williams, and since that time it has been used for various purposes including a school, a club, offices and shops. In the later part of the nineteenth century a second bay was added and, later, the ground floor was projected forward to incorporate a row of shops.

24. The Falcon

This beautiful old building sits on the corner of Grosvenor Street and Lower Bridge Street. It started life as a house in around 1200 and was later extended to the south along Lower Bridge Street, with a Great Hall running parallel to the street. During the thirteenth century it was rebuilt, leaving the Row in-situ. It was rebuilt again during the late sixteenth and early seventeenth centuries, and in 1602 it was bought by Sir Richard Grosvenor, who extensively altered it some forty years later to make it his town house. In 1643 Sir Richard petitioned the City Assembly for permission to enlarge the house by enclosing the portion of the Row which passed through his property. This was successful and it set a precedent for other residents in Lower Bridge Street to enclose their portion of the Rows, or to build new structures which did not incorporate the Rows. As a result that street no longer has conventional Rows, unlike most of the city centre.

The Falcon public house.

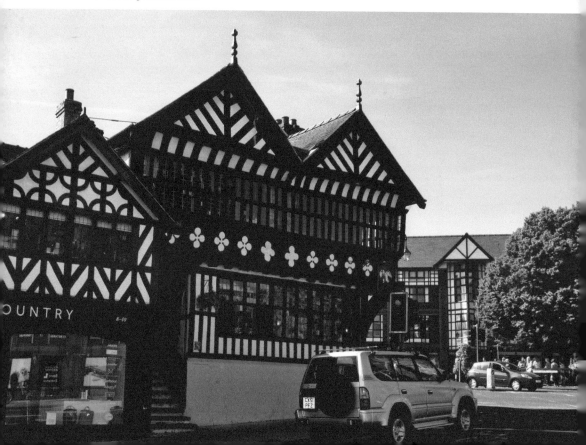

In the late eighteenth century the building ceased to be the town house of the Grosvenor family, although it continued to be owned by them, and between 1778 and 1878 it was licensed as The Falcon Inn. In the 1800s it was restored by John Douglas and The Falcon became the Falcon Cocoa House, serving only non-alcoholic drinks. During the 1960s the pub lay empty but it was later restored by The Falcon Trust after the Grosvenor family donated the building to them, and after a full restoration it was formally reopened by His Grace the Duke of Westminster in May 1992.

The Falcon in the 1950s.

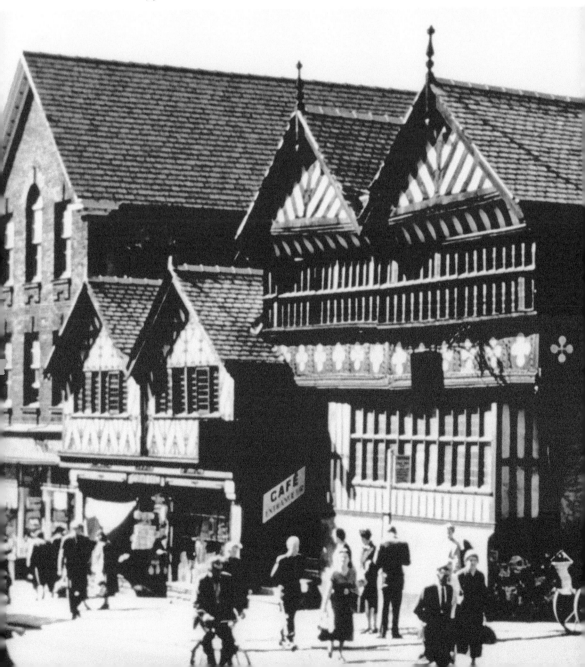

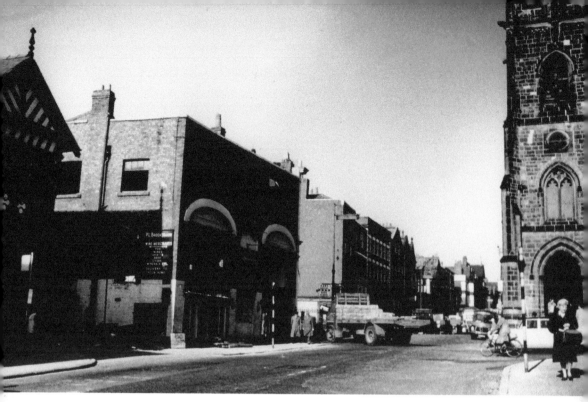

The Falcon in 1959 showing the junction before the ring road.

Beneath the pub is a medieval undercroft that is currently used as a beer cellar. The building is Grade I listed.

25. St Michael's Church

Sitting in the centre of Chester City at the junction of Bridge Street and Pepper Street is the redundant church of St Michael. This beautiful Grade II-listed building with its buff-coloured sandstone walls dates from around the fifteenth century and sits on the site of a church that was burnt down in the Great Fire of Chester in 1188. According to an account found in the churchwarden's register, it was almost completely rebuilt in 1582. Later, during the English Civil War, the church was used as a prison during the Siege of Chester. In 1709 the steeple was replaced by a stone tower. The church was never particularly well attended and had a rollercoaster ride of building, crumbling and rebuilding again. By 1839 it was felt prudent to amalgamate the parish into one, joining with St Olaf's at the bottom of Bridge Street, but by 1840 the interior had become dilapidated, with an unsafe tower. Between 1849 and 1841 the church was virtually rebuilt to the design of James Harrison. The church carried on with a dwindling congregation and by 1972 it's time was up: it was stripped of its furnishings and taken over by Chester City Council. In 1975 they reopened the church as the Chester Heritage Centre, the first heritage centre in the country. It is now controlled by the Cheshire West and Chester Council. The building stands on part of the Rows and can be accessed from them or from Bridge Street.

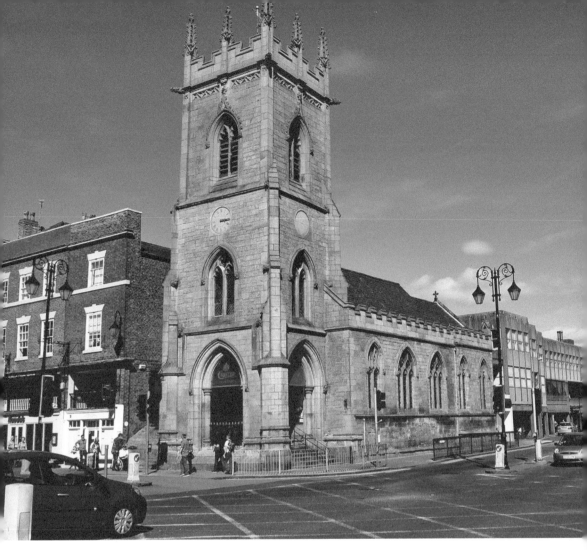

St Michael's Church.

26. The Three Old Arches

Almost opposite Chester Heritage Centre in Upper Bridge Street is our next building. The street is now pedestrianised and on the left, at No. 48 Bridge Street, is an ancient row of shops with the words 'Three Old Arches' on the front elevation and the date AD 1274. It was built in the thirteenth century and sometime later was joined to the building next door, No. 50, making it the largest townhouse on the Chester Rows. A large hall was incorporated into the buildings and this remains partly intact. The undercroft of No. 48 has had the stone columns removed and replaced with steel beams. The undercroft of No. 50 still retains its stone column. These shops are Grade I listed and at street level it is believed to be the oldest shop frontage still surviving in England today.

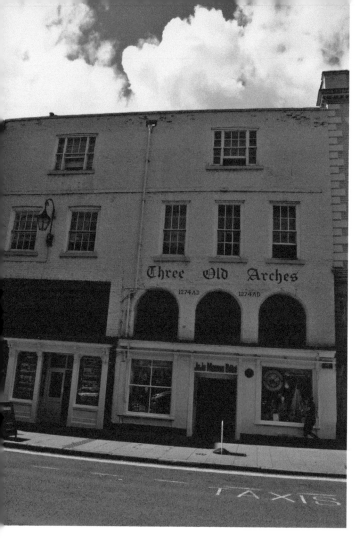

The Three Old Arches in Upper Bridge Street.

27. The Dutch Houses

Situated at Nos 22–26 Lower Bridge Street can be found what were once the tallest buildings in the street. They were built over undercrofts around 1665–70. Chester was still an important port at that time, although would not be for much longer, and it is thought that the name Dutch Houses relates to the trade carried out with the Low Countries – or it may simply be due to the original style of building. In the 1700s, however, there was a small Dutch community residing in Lower Bridge Street. The buildings are now three shops and have a section of the Chester Rows. They are Grade II listed and have been rebuilt over time. Chester architect Thomas Lockwood is reported as having restored it during 1873 but by 1947 the building still retained a considerable amount of its original architectural features. Like other similar large houses in the city it went through a period of neglect and by the 1970s was in danger of collapse. The City Council stepped in and rescued the buildings, although with a less than sympathetic rebuild: the whole of the front façade was removed and replaced and interior work was carried out, including the exchange of heavy wooden beams for metal ones. At least it wasn't demolished!

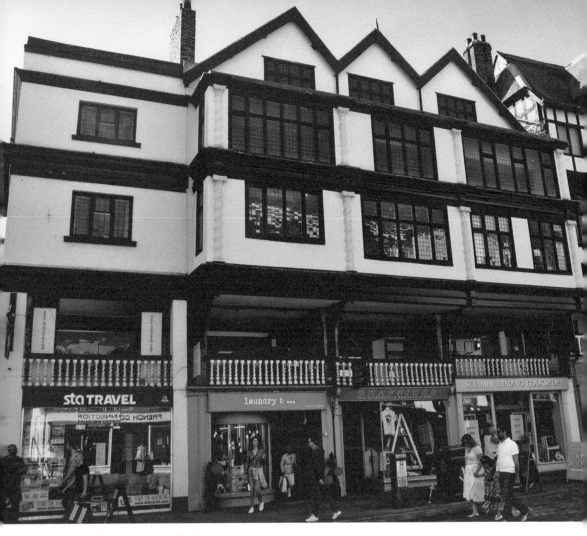

The Dutch Houses in Bridge Street.

28. No. 1 Bridge Street

Continuing to the top of Bridge Street, in the area known as The Cross, is No. 1 Bridge Street. This beautiful black-and-white Revival building is situated on the corner of Bridge Street and Eastgate Street. It incorporates part of the Chester Rows and while architectural purists may be critical of these buildings – which only date from the late 1800s – these relatively modern buildings add so much to Chester's charm.

The building was designed by Thomas Meakin (T. M.) Lockwood for the 1st Duke of Westminster but the following year it was owned by Chester City Council. The building is reputed locally to be one of Lockwood's most beautiful works planned in his own flamboyant style.

This building was erected in 1888 after the older one was so decrepit that it had to be demolished. In the National Heritage List for England it is Grade II listed, and well deserves its place as one of Chester's most noteworthy buildings.

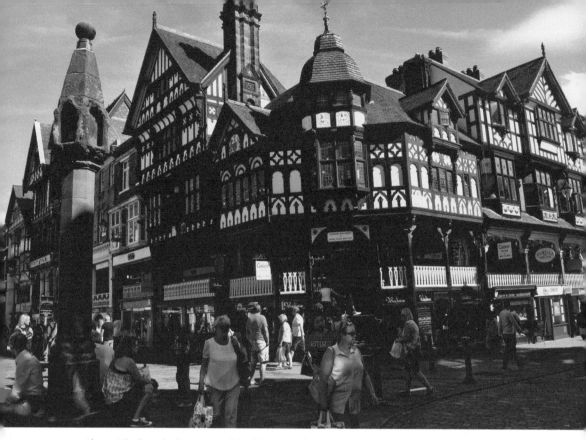

Above: Black-and-white Revival buildings at The Cross.

Below: The buildings originally there.

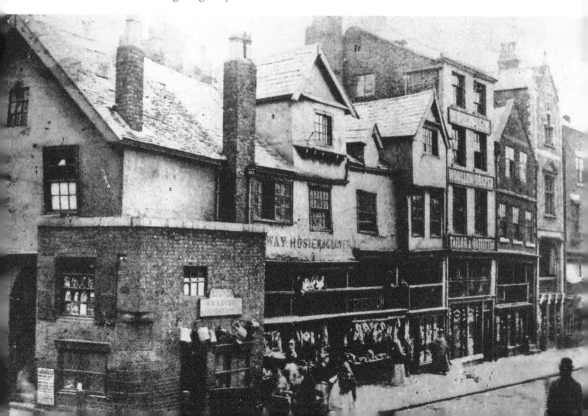

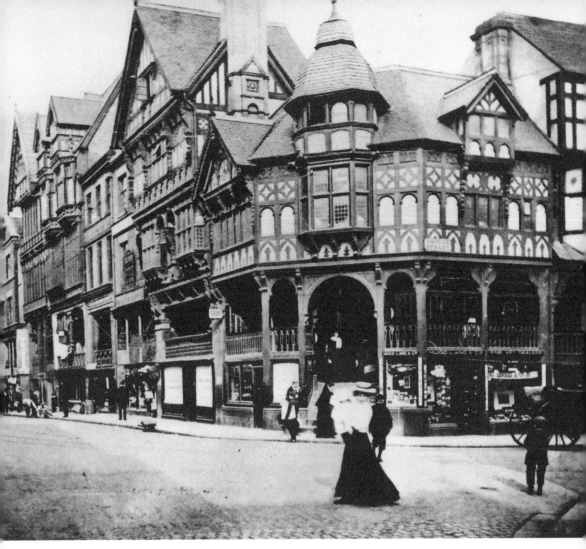

The buildings in the early 1900s.

29. The Commercial Coffee Rooms

Continuing past The Cross and into Northgate Street, the first building on the left after the narrow entry leading to St Paul's churchyard are The Commercial Coffee Rooms. This building is situated at no. 1 Northgate Street and was designed by Thomas Harrison and built in 1807 as a gentleman's club. It became known as The Commercial Coffee Room and later the Commercial Newsroom. In 1815 the contents of the City Library found their temporary home here but the books were later transferred to the Mechanics' Institute to await a more permanent home in the new City Library in 1877. The Newsroom had its own committee and at the time its members included the mayor, local MPs and senior military officers. Since the middle of the nineteenth century it has been known as The Chester City Club, one of the oldest gentleman's clubs in the country. At the time of writing it is a branch of the Skipton Building Society. Entry to the club is from St Peter's churchyard, where the Commercial Hotel, built in the same year as the Coffee Rooms, also can be found.

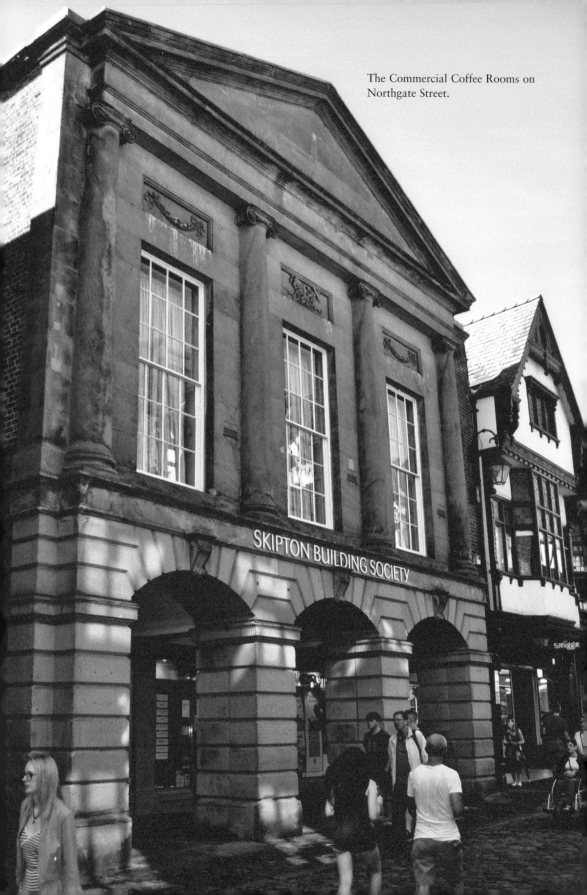

The Commercial Coffee Rooms on Northgate Street.

30. Nos 3–31 Northgate Street

The row of attractive terraced buildings in Northgate Street were individually designed by H.W. Beswick, John Douglas and James Strong. Nos 15 and 17 were designed by James Strong in 1909, the latter as a pub, the Cross Keys Inn. In the cellar of No. 23 can be seen the remains of the columns from the Principia of the Roman fort that once occupied the site. Number 25 was formally the Woolpack Inn, which was rebuilt by John Douglas in 1903 and modernised in 1914 by James Strong. Nos 27–31 are a bit more complex, being on the corner with views into both Northgate Street and the Town Square. The whole row was re-faced in black-and-white by John Douglas in 1902.

The Dublin Packet pub, round the corner in Town Square, is part of this beautiful row of buildings. This cosy pub has now been half hidden by the questionable rebuilding that took place some time ago. The pub is shown in the 1829 directory. It is believed that the name comes from the time when a regular packet boat would leave Chester docks for Dublin. There was a famous licensee later in the pub's life: a gentleman by the name of William Ralph 'Dixie' Dean had a glowing football career and played for many teams, notably

Nos 3–31 Northgate Street.

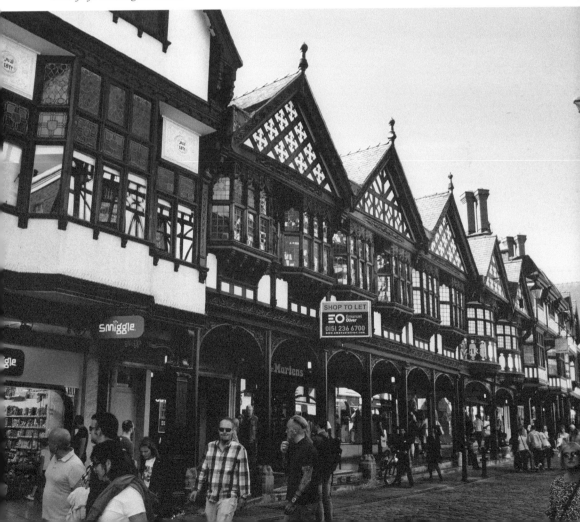

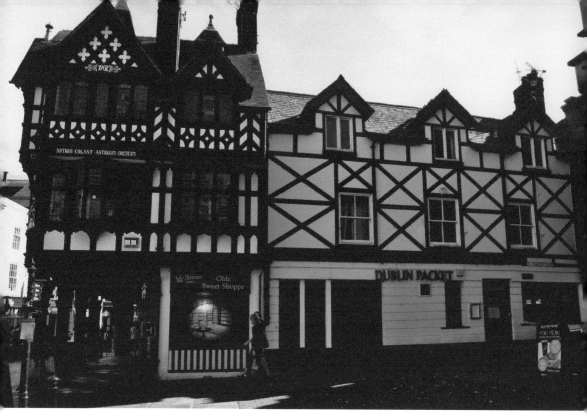

The Dublin Packet.

Everton, when he was known as England's greatest goal scorer. His international debut came playing for England against Wales at the racecourse ground in Wrexham in 1927, just after he turned twenty. The result was a 3-3 draw, with Dixie scoring twice. During his international career he won sixteen England caps and scored eighteen goals for England.

Dixie Dean followed up an exceptionally successful career in football as a shopkeeper of sports goods in Birkenhead, but only for a short while. Then came the Second World War and Dixie was called up; he had a good army career playing and managing service football as well as being a corporal mechanic. Shortly after the war, this football legend took over the Dublin Packet and remained there for around sixteen years. Even then he continued to play, this time for the Northgate Brewery team. This was the heyday of the Dublin Packet, a very happy pub that was constantly visited by the famous and not so famous paying homage to the great man. Believe it or not, at the time of writing this iconic Chester pub is now closed.

31. The Town Hall

The Chester Town Hall has had a varied history. In 1698 an Exchange was built for the city's administrators but this building burnt down in 1862. A competition was held to build a new Town Hall and this was won by William Henry Lynn of Belfast. The building was officially opened on 15 October 1869 by the Prince of Wales (the future Edward VII), who was accompanied by Mr William Gladstone, the prime minister. On 27 March 1897, the Council Chamber on the second floor was gutted by fire and it was restored by T. M. Lockwood the following year.

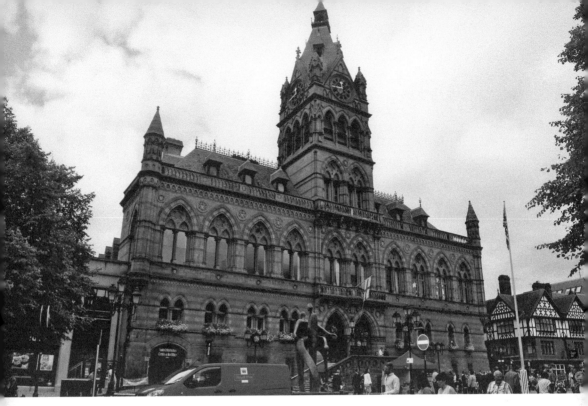

The Town Hall.

For many years until 1967 Chester's main police station was situated on the Town Hall's ground floor. Chester originally had its own police force, the Chester City Police, under its own Chief Constable. The old police station's cells in the Town Hall still exist, as does the old Magistrates' Court or Quarter Sessions of the City of Chester that were held in this court until the abolition of Quarter Sessions by the Courts Act 1971. From then until 1993 it was used as a Magistrates' Court, with the adjoining room as a retiring room for the magistrates. One of the remaining original Victorian courts in the country, it has featured in such films as *Sherlock Holmes* (2009) and *Far from the Madding Crowd* (2015).

The work that had been undertaken at the Town Hall is now carried out at the council offices and this beautiful building is used for such things as weddings and events. It remains, however, a symbol of Chester.

32. The Coachworks

The original bus station was situated beside the attractive terracotta and red-brick Westminster Coach and Motor Car Works building, with its elaborately moulded terracotta and red-brick façade. This most attractive of buildings was built in 1913 to a design by Philip Lockwood to house a coach-building workshops and motor showroom. Cars were sold from the showrooms up until the 1970s. It was rebuilt in 1981–84, retaining the original façade, to become the new home of the Chester Library. (The first public library in Chester dated back to the City Library in Whitefriars in 1773.) The Chester Library has now moved to the former Chester Odeon, now the Storyhouse in Hunter Street, leaving this building to enjoy another lease of life, possibly as a market.

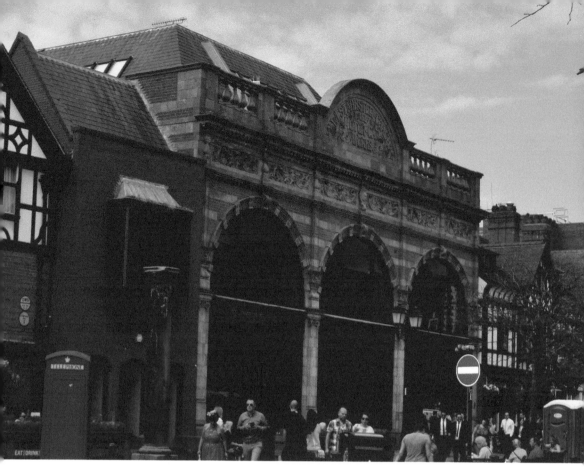

Above: The former coachworks.

Below: The old market hall, 1890s.

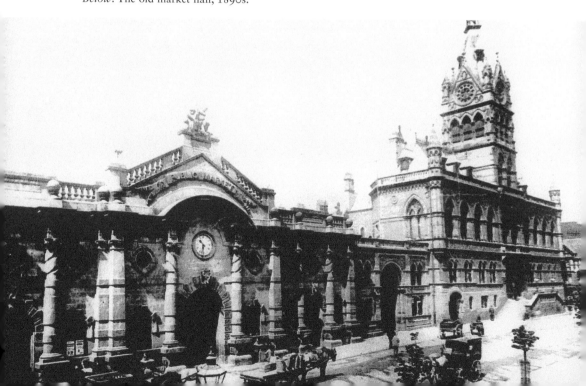

33. The Abbey Gateway

Across the road from Northgate Street and the Market Place we find the ancient Abbey Gateway, giving access to Chester Cathedral. It leads through to Abbey Square and is a Grade I-listed building. It was built as a gatehouse to what was then the Abbey of St Werburgh in the fourteenth century and rebuilt around 1800. There is a large arched gateway with a pedestrian gate and on either side are niches for religious effigies. The upper building is described as a robing room and a court room for pleas of the abbey and the Bishop's Registry. It was built atop the gate during the Georgian period (1714–1830). A more macabre story concerning the Abbey Gateway is that Sir Thomas Featherstonehaugh was, in 1651, beheaded in front of the gateway, having been charged with contacting the Royalist cause during the Civil War.

When built, the Abbey Gateway led to the grounds of the monastery, which had, in those early days, a brewery and bakehouse. There was also a small lake known as the Horse Pool and on New Year's Eve 1523 the gatekeeper fell in and drowned. It was filled in during the late 1500s and the area became a green.

In the eighteenth century a column from the Exchange building (which burnt down and replaced by the Town Hall) was erected upon it and still stands there to this day. The area is known as Abbey Square or Abbey Green and once housed the Kings School. This prestigious school was situated in buildings adjoining the north-west corner of the Cathedral. These dedicated school buildings were opened by William Gladstone in 1876. During the 1940s pupil numbers rose and the school took over part of the former Bluecoat School buildings on Upper Northgate Street. By the early 1950s, a 999-year lease had been secured with the Eaton Estate for the current 32-acre site on Wrexham Road, on the outskirts of the city. Design of the buildings started in 1956, and in 1960 the whole school moved to the new site.

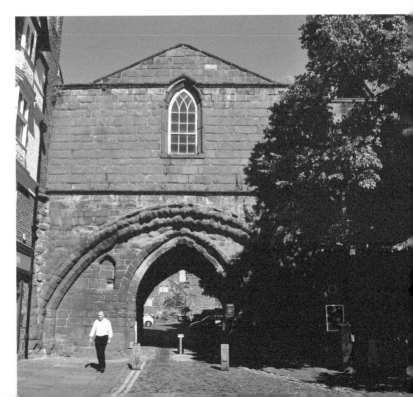

The Abbey Gateway to Chester Cathedral.

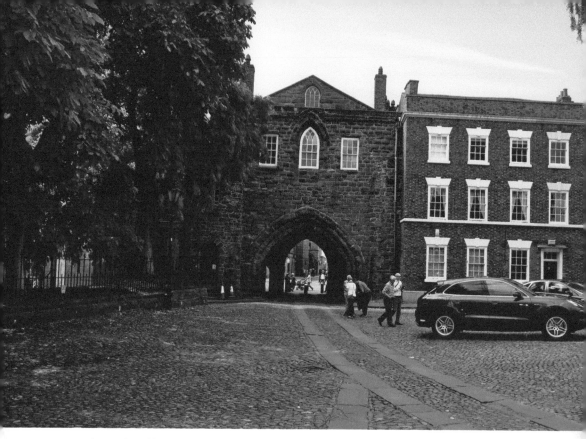

Above: The Abbey Gateway to Chester Cathedral, from within.

Below: Column from the Exchange building.

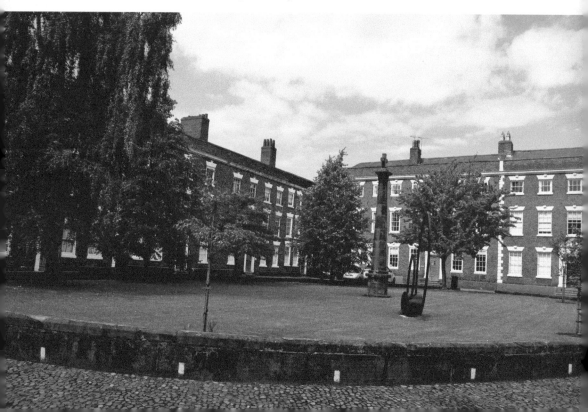

34. The Coach House Inn

Continuing past the Town Hall in the Market Square we find an old pub that for a while was closed and boarded up! Fortunately, this did not last and it is now once again open and called The Coach House Inn. Situated almost opposite Chester Cathedral and next to the Town Hall, it is shown in the Chester Directory of 1781 as a pub called the Coach and Horses in Northgate Street with the licensee being a Mr Davies. In 1872 the building front was remodelled in mock-Tudor style by students of James Harrison, but the fabric of the building dates from the early seventeenth century. It stands near the site of the White Lion, a noted coaching pub, but the Coach and Horses was itself a notable pub where stagecoaches would stop on their way to all points of the compass. Now, the inn is once again open and continues to sit proudly on Chester's Market Square.

The Coach House Inn.

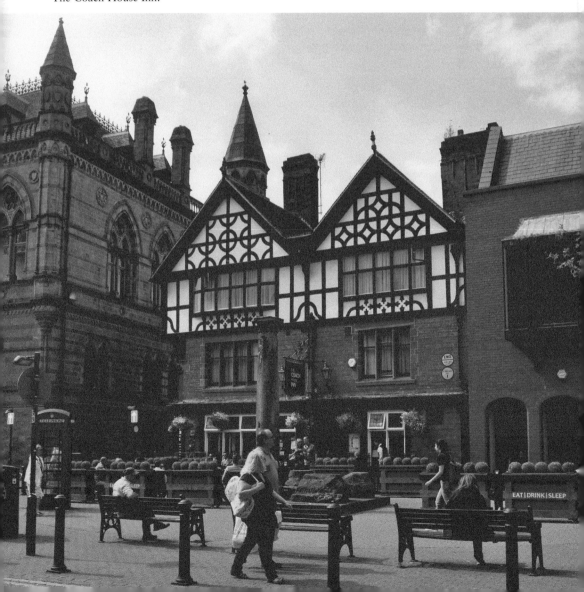

35. The Blue Bell

The former Blue Bell Inn at Nos 63–65 Northgate Street is possibly the oldest domestic structure in Chester; it dates from the mid- to late fifteenth century but could very well be older. The braced roof points to a construction date of between 1250 and 1400, although parts of the building may date back to the eleventh century. It formed part of Lorimers Row, an ancient group of buildings with an arcade at ground level. 'Lorimer' is a Scottish word meaning a maker and seller of spurs and horse tackle made from metal. It is justifiably one of Chester's Grade I-listed buildings.

The first licence to serve alcoholic drink was issued in 1494, making it the oldest surviving example of a medieval inn. If you look carefully at the old photograph you will see a small square hole in the upper part, this was level with the top of carriages and was used to sell tickets to those riding there. Successive councils had proved unwilling to spend money on conservation. In 1959, for example, the Corporation announced that the building was in such a poor state that it was to be pulled down. The ensuing campaign ended when the government refused to permit demolition, and in the early 1960s the Corporation had to spend £2,500 on preserving the building.

This ancient pub has the pavement running through the ground floor of the building; it originally consisted of two medieval houses which were joined together in the eighteenth century.

The name Blue Bell could relate to the proximity of the pub to the Abbey and the 'curfew bell' in the bell-yard. The bell was rung to warn 'strangers' to leave the city before the gates were closed at 8 p.m. Today it is currently a successful tapas restaurant and bar which goes by the name Blue Bell 1494, after the year that it started serving alcoholic drinks.

An old photo of the Blue Bell Inn.

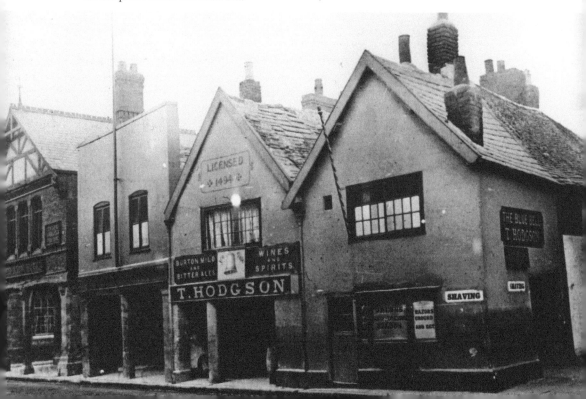

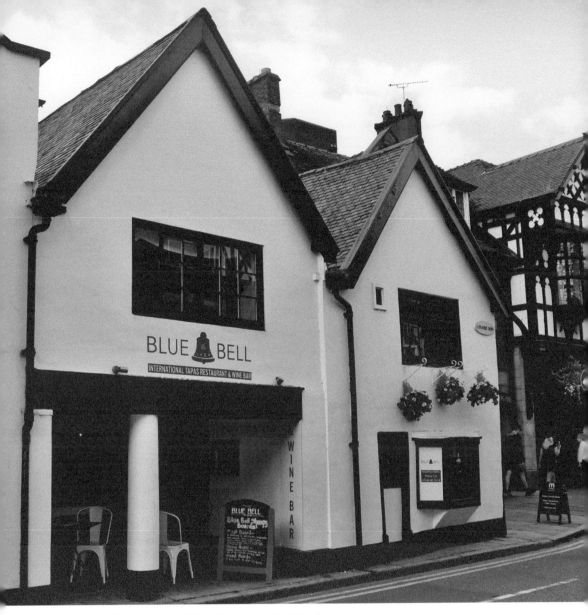

The Blue Bell International Tapas Restaurant & Wine Bar.

36. The Pied Bull

Passing the Blue Bell, we come to probably the oldest continuously licensed pub in Chester. It was built sometime in the thirteenth century as a mansion house going by the name of Bull Mansion. The land on which it was built was given to the Nuns of St Mary, and dwelling houses were built here in 1267. It has a handmade staircase dating back to 1533, when it was rebuilt and became the home of the Recorder of Chester. Around twenty years later it became an inn and was called The Bull Inn, reflecting the existence of the cattle or beast market outside the nearby Northgate; this was later changed to The Pied Bull, which became one of Chester's important coaching inns.

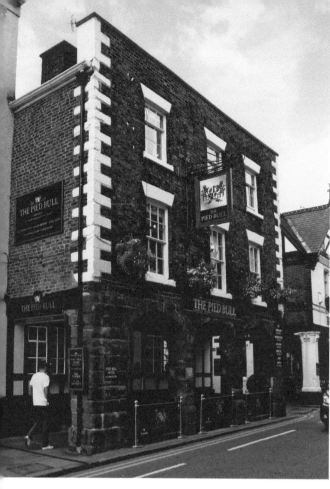

Left: The Pied Bull.

Below: The Pied Bull interior.

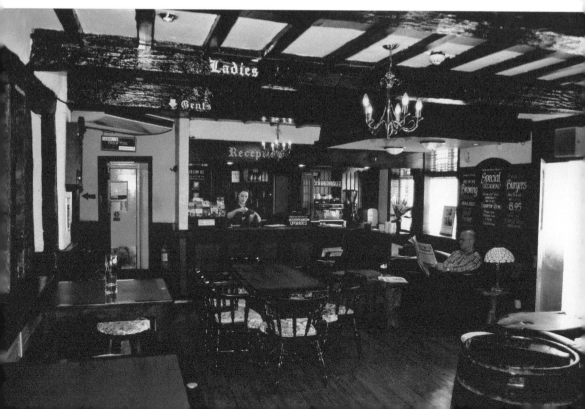

It remains on what was the extensive Lorimers Row but that now only stretches from The Pied Bull to the Blue Bell. In 1660, it was largely rebuilt and then again in the mid-1700s when it received the brickwork style that we see today, although it is still a timber framed building dating from the year that it was built. In 1828, it was recorded as a hotel with Mr Thomas as the licensee. It is filled with period charm and has been tastefully and carefully modernised through the years. The staircase dates from 1533 and it is a designated Grade II-listed building.

37. The Northgate and Gaol

We continue to the Northgate, which once housed Chester's notorious gaol. It was an enormous gateway described by the historian Hemmingway as 'an inconvenient and unseemly pile of buildings'. Although standing on sandstone, it had dungeons cut into it, forming dank and dreary cells. As some of the prisoners kept there were unlikely to walk free again it was not a pleasant ending to a life. It was described in the seventeenth century as a 'dark stinking place with a dead man's room'. It was here that prisoners from all over Cheshire were kept prior to execution. Torture was also carried out here, and one of the cells was so small that it was torture to even be in it, hence its name 'Little Ease'. Public flogging and transportation to Australia were alternative punishments for the 'lucky' prisoners.

The Northgate and gaol.

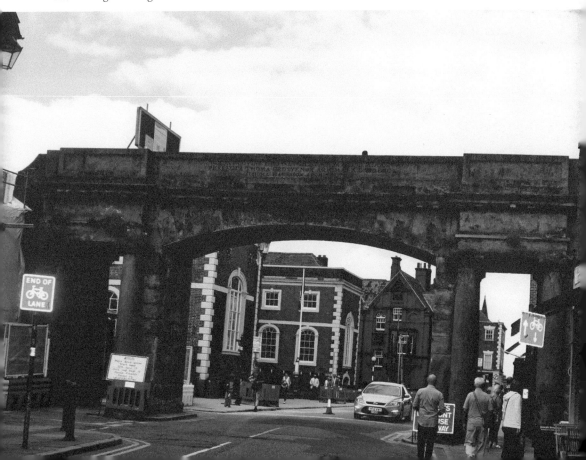

Take a peep out of the old gateway and look through the railings above the canal. On the left in Upper Northgate Street is The Bridge of Sighs, another Grade II listed structure. Designed by the architect Joseph Turner and built in around 1793, it was a crossing that led from the Northgate gaol across the Chester Canal to the Little St John Chapel in the Bluecoat School, where condemned prisoners would receive the last rites in a 'special room' before returning to the gaol to meet the executioner and be 'turned off', meaning to be hanged. When built, this narrow and flimsy-looking bridge had high railings on it to prevent prisoners from attempting to pre-empt the executioner.

In 1801, all executions took place at Gallows Hill in Boughton but after that date they were delivered to the Northgate until the City Gaol and House of Correction was erected in 1807. Overlooking the Roodee, this took on the duties of the Northgate gaol until 1878, when it was closed and prisoners delivered to the gaol in the castle. The land later became a girls' school. In 1808, the Northgate gaol and gate were taken down and in 1810, the present gate was designed by Thomas Harrison. This is now a Grade I-listed building.

The Bridge of Sighs.

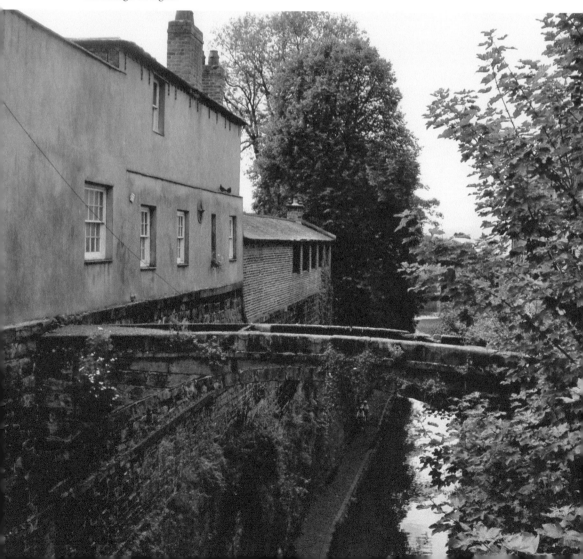

38. The Bluecoat School

Continuing through the Northgate, the first building that we come to is the Bluecoat School. Before the school was built it was the site of the medieval hospital of St John the Baptist, which was established by Ranulph Blundeville between 1180 and 1200. Like a lot of buildings across Britain, this school building suffered during the English Civil War and was substantially destroyed. In 1717 this school was established by Dr Nicholas Stratford, Lord Bishop of Chester from 1689 to 1707, and built for a charity called the Society for Promoting Christian Knowledge. It was originally L-shaped but in 1733 a north wing was added. The south wing faces the city walls and it is here that the school chapel could be found. As previously mentioned, this chapel was also used to give the last rights to prisoners from the Northgate goal who were condemned to death. The main wing contained the classrooms and the dormitories and in 1854 the front façade was updated. At the same time a statue of John Coppack, a pupil of the school, was installed above the main entrance, where he can still be seen in his smart blue suit. Almshouses were originally built on land behind the school and these have been updated a few times, the last ones were new-builds in 2006, making them the first almshouses to be built since the 1800s.

In 1949 the school closed and, surprisingly for such a prestigious building, was left derelict for a while. It went through various uses until 1996, when it was taken over by the University of Chester as the new home for the history department.

The Bluecoat School.

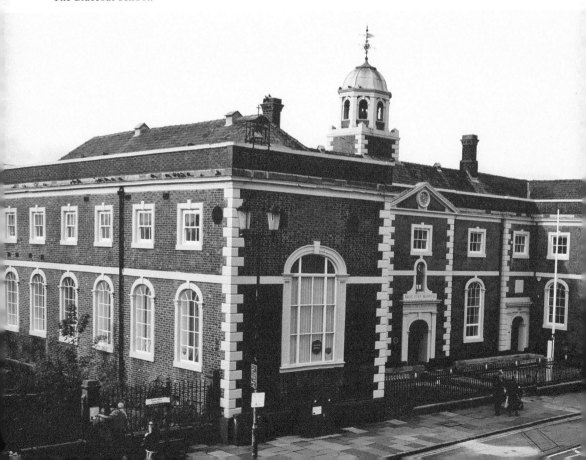

39. Chester Cathedral

Chester Cathedral is the mother church of the Diocese of Chester and is in the centre of the city. Since 1541 the cathedral, dedicated to Christ and the Blessed Virgin Mary has been the seat of the Bishop of Chester. The cathedral is a Grade I-listed building, and part of a heritage site that also includes the former monastic buildings to the north, which are also listed Grade I listed. Much of the interior is in Norman style and is the best example of eleventh- and twelfth-century church architecture in Cheshire. The cathedral has been modified many times from 1093 through to the sixteenth century, although the site itself may have been used for Christian worship since Roman times. All the major styles of English medieval architecture, from Norman to Perpendicular, are represented in the present building.

The cathedral and former monastic buildings were extensively restored during the nineteenth century, although perhaps not as efficiently as they could have been. The buildings are a major tourist attraction in Chester. In addition to holding services for Christian worship, the cathedral is used as a venue for concerts and exhibitions. Also in the cathedral is a memorial to John Travers Cornwell who, as a sixteen-year-old boy seaman aboard HMS *Chester*, was part of a gun crew during the Battle of Jutland in 1916. All the crew were killed and he remained at his post until he too was killed. He was awarded a posthumous Victoria Cross, the third youngest serviceman to be so honoured. (The man in charge of his squadron was Vice Admiral David Richard Beatty from Stapely, near Nantwich.)

Chester Cathedral in 1902.

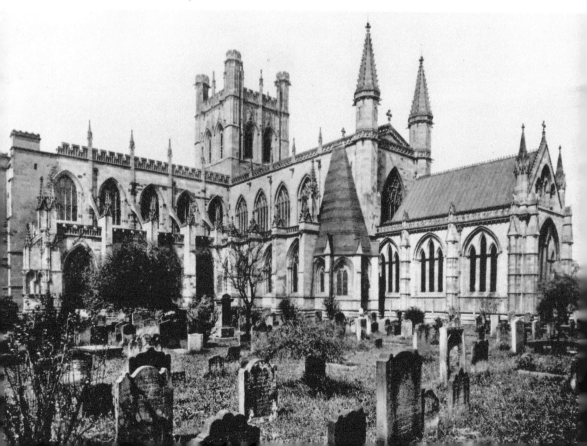

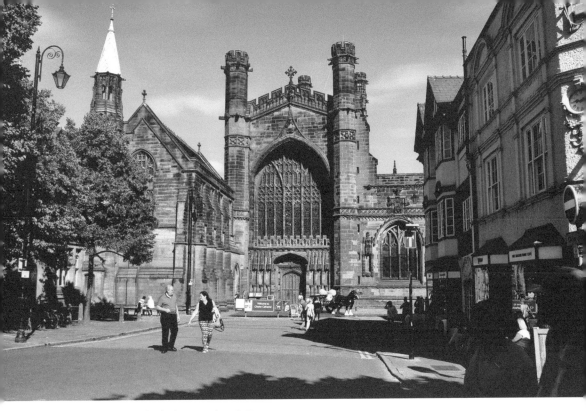

Above: Chester Cathedral, St Werburgh Street.

Below: Chester Cathedral showing the tribute to the Mercian Regiment in the form of a medal and ribbon.

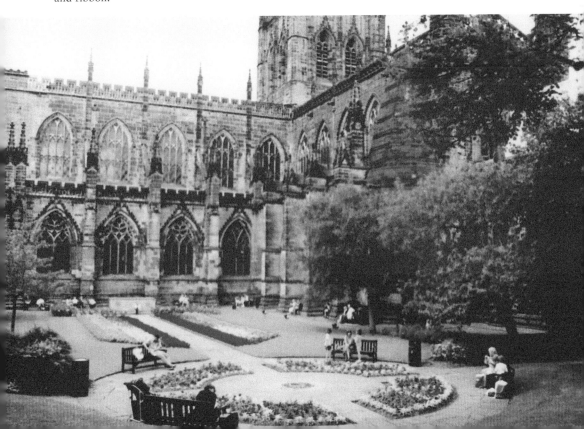

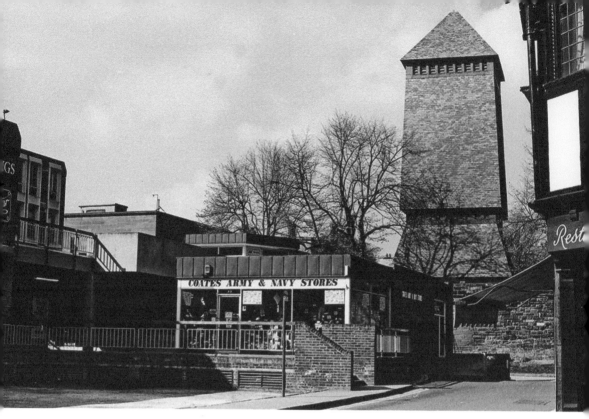

Chester Cathedral bell tower.

When the integral bell tower became unserviceable a rather incongruous free-standing bell tower was erected in the churchyard. It was named Addleshaw Tower after the Dean, the Revd G. W. O. Addleshaw, and designed by the architect to York Minster, George Pace. It was built in 1973, when the foundation stone was laid on 16 June by the Lord Lieutenant of Cheshire, Lord Leverhulme. It is the first free-standing bell tower built in the grounds of an English cathedral since the fifteenth century.

40. The Music Hall Cinema

In around 1280, when the present cathedral was still a monastery, the abbot, Simon de Albo, had a purpose-built chapel constructed and dedicated to St Nicholas. For many years the townspeople had been using the south aisle of the abbey as their parish, dedicated to St Oswald. With the rebuilding of the abbey's nave in the fourteenth century, the townspeople were required by the monks to move across the road to the former guild chapel of St Nicholas. This new accommodation seems to have been unpopular with the parishioners from the start as they later returned to worship in the south transept of the abbey, which was walled off from the rest of the great building and remained so until the late nineteenth century.

After remaining empty for a time, the old chapel was later used as a wool hall. It had also served as the Common Hall between 1545 and 1698. From 1773 it was called The New Theatre until it was renamed The Theatre Royal in 1777, where appeared such superstars of their day as Sarah Siddons in 1786 and Edmund Kean in 1815. Both an Act of Parliament and the personal assent of the monarch were necessary to obtain a licence to open a public theatre and copies of that pertaining to Chester still exist dating from the early part of the reign of George III in 1761. Licensing was deemed necessary because eighteenth-century theatres were seen by the authorities as hives of public disorder and potential unrest. Frequenting them could be found drunks, vagabonds, ladies of the night: basically the worst elements of society. Audiences didn't sit quietly to enjoy a nice play as they do today, but would argue and fight amongst themselves and throw objects and shout abuse at the performers if their efforts failed to please. Of the Act relating to Chester, it is

Music Hall cinema, St Werburgh Street.

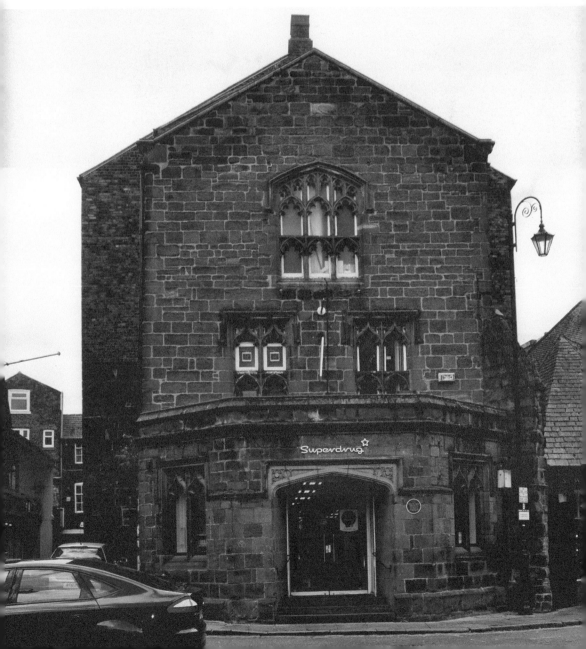

interesting to note that it was allied to an Act of Queen Anne for 'reducing the laws relating to Rogues, Vagabonds, Sturdy Beggars and Vagrants'.

The theatre remained a source of official suspicion and plays were required to be licensed by the Lord Chancellor right up to the 1960s. In 1855 the building became the home of the Chester Music Hall, after being redesigned by architect James Harrison.

Charles Dickens gave a talk here in 1867 and later described it thus: 'The hall is like a Methodist Chapel in low spirits, and with a cold in its head.' Many other famous names gave lectures here, including the explorer Roald Amundsen, and Winston Churchill, who spoke on the Boer War in 1901. Films were shown occasionally from the early part of the twentieth century. The London Animated Picture Co. ran films here in 1908. Films were screened on a regular basis from 1915, when it was known as Music Hall Pictures. Chester Music Hall (1921) Ltd reconstructed the hall and ran the cinema from 1921. The screen was moved from the St Werburgh Street end to the Northgate end. The first film shown was Charlie Chaplin's *The Kid*, opening in November 1921. Chester's first 'talkie', *The Singing Fool* starring Al Jolson, was seen at the Music Hall on 23 September 1929.

In April 1961 the Music Hall closed. The final offering was the romantic comedy *Never on Sunday*. Since closure the building has been many things, including a branch of Lipton's (Chester's first supermarket within the walls), Foster's gent's outfitters and The Reject Shop. It is currently home to a branch of Superdrug.

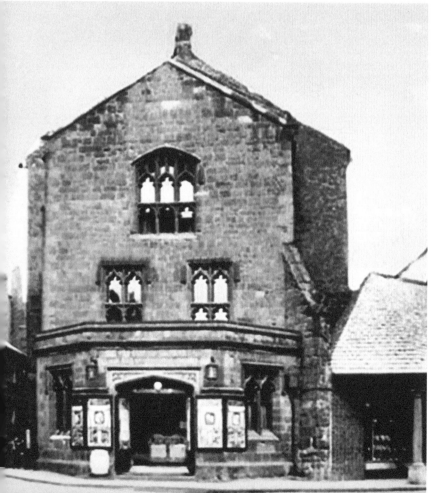

An old photo of the Music Hall on St Werburgh Street.

41. Nos 2–18 St Werburgh Street

Continuing along St Werburgh Street past Chester Cathedral and following the road round to the right we are faced with a beautiful street of black-and-white mock-Tudor buildings. This part of St Werburgh Street was once half its width until it was widened and the east side redeveloped by the Corporation with the backing of the Duke of Westminster and the designs of architect John Douglas. A row of shops was demolished and the council wanted to build replacements and sell them individually. John Douglas, however, purchased the whole row himself prior to building and wanted to build it in another of his favourite styles, red brick. The Duke intervened and asked him to build it in his trademark black-and-white mock-Tudor style, a request that Douglas complied with. The row was built between 1895 and 1897 at a cost of around £17,000 (roughly £1,800,000 in today's money).

On the wall at the bottom of the street we see a plaque honouring the man responsible for a lot, but not all, of the black-and-white buildings in Chester, namely John Douglas. The famous Cheshire architect came from Sandiway, near Northwich, and his superb works can be found across the county and further afield.

The first of the new buildings to be occupied was the one on the corner of Eastgate Street, built for and occupied by the Bank of Liverpool; the other units were used as shops. If you look up at the front of this beautiful building you will see evidence of the words Bank of Liverpool. This bank was founded in 1831 and in 1918 it acquired Martins bank and the name changed to Bank of Liverpool and Martins Ltd. The name was shortened to Martins Bank in 1928. In 1969 it was acquired by Barclays Bank, and its 700 branches all became Barclays. It currently houses Sole Trader shoe shop.

Nos 2–18 St Werburgh Street.

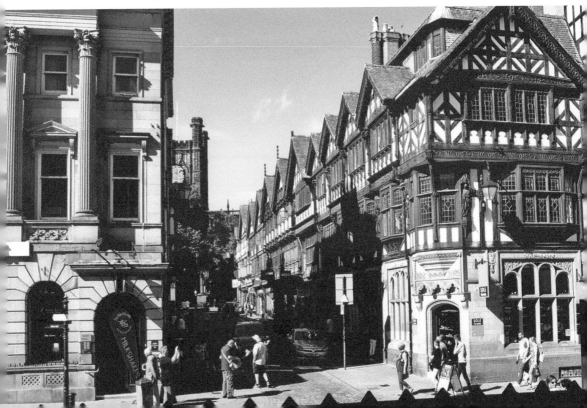

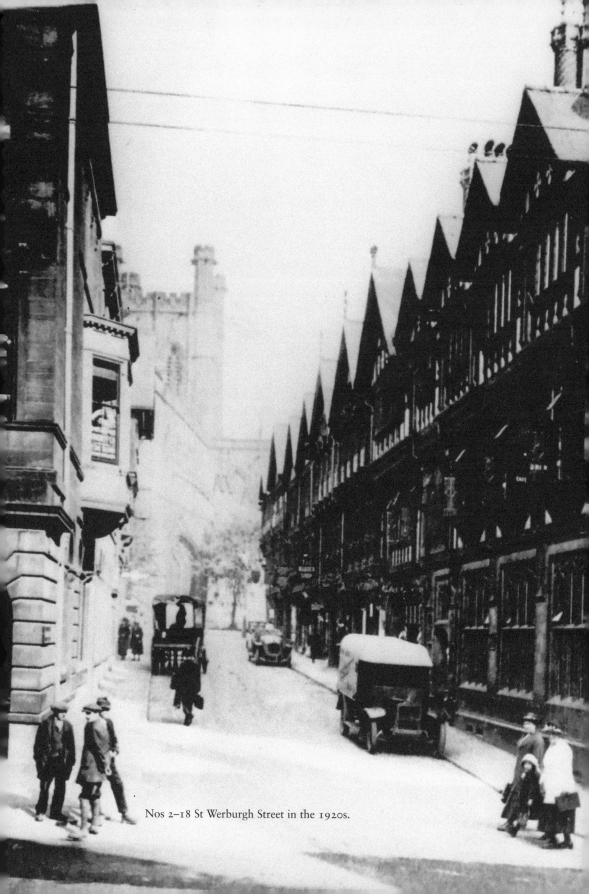

Nos 2–18 St Werburgh Street in the 1920s.

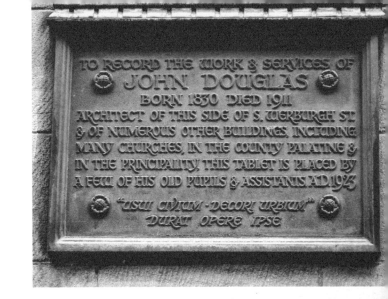

Right: John Douglas plaque.

Below: Sole Trader shop.

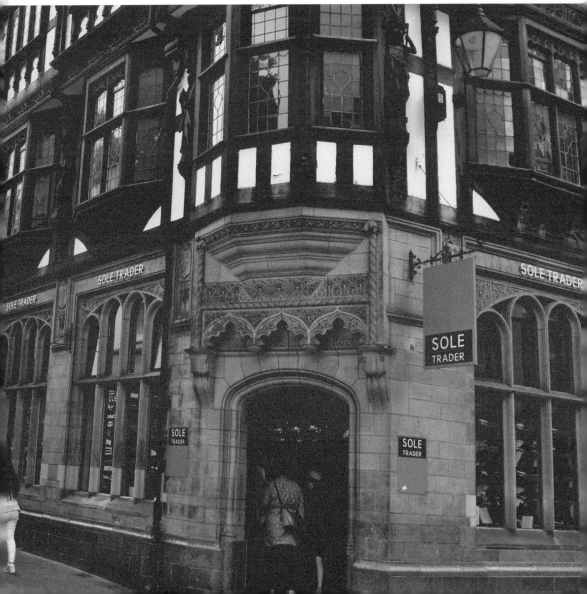

42. Chester Eastgate

Leaving St Werburgh Street and entering Eastgate Street we are faced with another gate out of the city – the Eastgate with its famous clock. This clock is said to be the second most photographed in England after Big Ben. It was designed by the architect John Douglas to celebrate Queen Victoria's Diamond Jubilee in 1897 and was built by the cousin of John Douglas, James Swindley of Handbridge. The clock itself was provided by J. B. Joyce and Company Ltd of Whitchurch.

During the early years it had to be wound by hand every week and by the early 1950s the clock needed repairing. J. B. Joyce agreed to dismantle and overhaul the clock in September 1953 for the sum of £50.

The original gate was guarded by a timber tower – this was replaced by a stone one in the second century. This gate was demolished in around the fourteenth century and replaced with another one. The present gate dates from 1768. From the top you can view two of Chester's main streets, Foregate Street to the left and Eastgate Street to the right. Eastgate Street is now mainly pedestrianised but in the days when traffic used it there was much congestion.

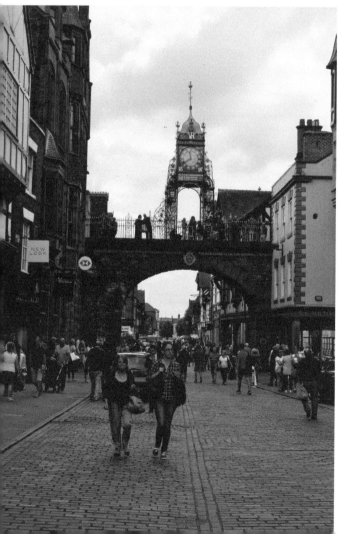

Chester Eastgate.

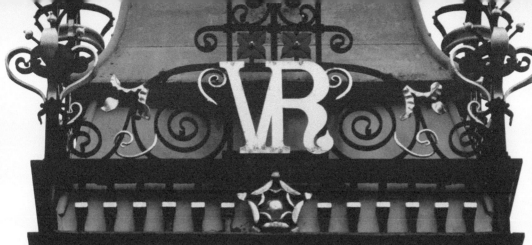

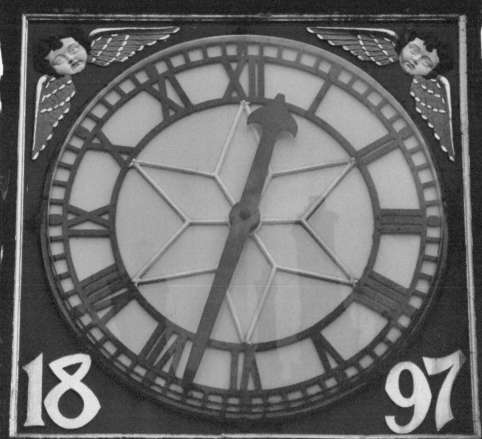

VR

18 97

THIS CLOCK WAS PRESENTED
TO THE CITY BY
EDWARD EVANS-LLOYD
CITIZEN & FREEMAN. 1897.

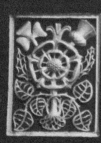

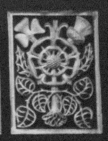

Eastgate Clock.

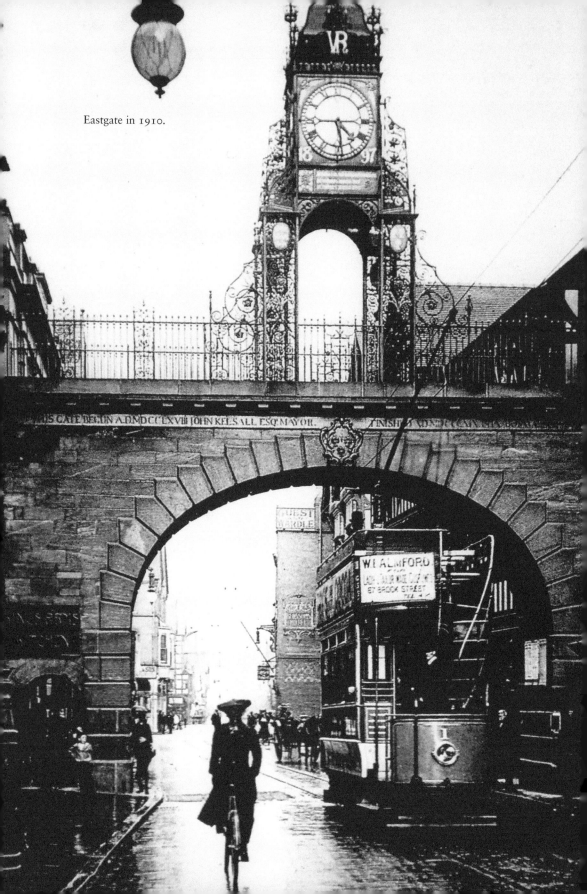

Eastgate in 1910.

43. The Grosvenor Hotel

Next to the Eastgate is Chester's top hotel, The Grosvenor, a name that you will come across in many parts of Chester. Gerald Grosvenor, 6th Duke of Westminster, lived in Chester at Eaton Hall until his untimely death in 2016. His son, Hugh Grosvenor, now assumes the title 7th Duke of Westminster.

Grosvenor is the Duke of Westminster's family name, which explains such features in the city as the Grosvenor Bridge and Grosvenor Park. Much of Chester's architecture dates from the Victorian era, with many of the buildings being modelled on Jacobean architecture, with its half-timbered style and with many exceptions, designed by Cheshire architect John Douglas, who was employed by the duke as his principal architect. His trademark was twisted chimney stacks, many of which can be seen on buildings in the city centre. Another feature of the buildings belonging to the estate of Westminster is the 'Grey Diamonds' – a weaving pattern of grey bricks in the red brickwork laid out in a diamond formation.

The Grosvenor Hotel, as it was called in the 1950s, is now known as The Chester Grosvenor and is a Grade II-listed building built between 1863 and 1866. It is owned by the Duke of Westminster. Before the present building was constructed the site was occupied first by the Golden Talbot pub and later by The Royal Hotel. The Golden Talbot was recorded as being 'ancient' in its 1751 mention in one of the local weekly newspapers and was in

The Grosvenor Hotel, 2010.

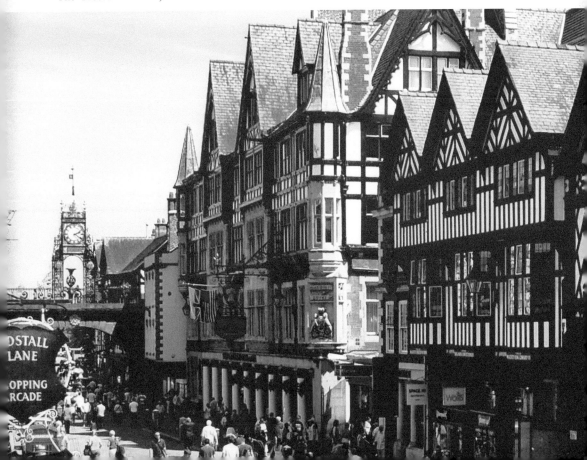

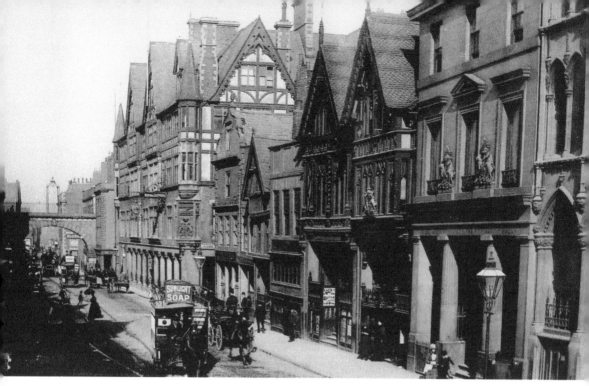

The Grosvenor Hotel in 1897.

operation during the reign of Elizabeth I. In 1784 the pub was demolished to make way for The Royal Hotel, built by the politician and landowner the 1st Baron Crewe. It became the headquarters of the Independent Party, who were opposed to the Grosvenor family, later to become the Dukes of Westminster. In 1815 it was purchased by Robert Grosvenor, who was at that time Earl Grosvenor and who later became the 1st Marquess of Westminster. It was then renamed the Grosvenor Hotel, the city's 'premier place to stay'. While it was in the possession of the 1st Marquess' son, Richard Grosvenor, in 1863, the building was demolished and the building now present on the site, again originally called the Grosvenor Hotel, was built. It was designed by the Chester architect Thomas Mainwaring Penson and was his last major work. It was completed after his death by his son's firm, R. K. Penson & Ritchie. The hotel passed into the estate of the Duke of Westminster when Richard's son, Hugh Grosvenor, was advanced to 1st Duke of Westminster in 1874.

44. Crypt Chambers

A magnificent building called Crypt Chambers is situated at Nos 34–40 Eastgate Row. Designed by T. M. Penson, it is a Grade I-listed building and is built on the site of a house whose undercroft is still present and in use. The building incorporates part of the Chester Rows. On the front of the tower at Row level is a blank scroll, on the east face is a recessed panel containing the initials W. B. (for William Brown), on the west face the initials are C.B. (for Charles Brown) and on the rear face is a scroll inscribed AD 1858: Crypt Chambers. The gothic façade frontage is built over a medieval undercroft dating from the twelfth century. The undercroft currently contains the Tea Press tearoom and the architectural historian Nikolaus Pevsner considered this undercroft to be 'one of the best medieval crypts of Chester'.

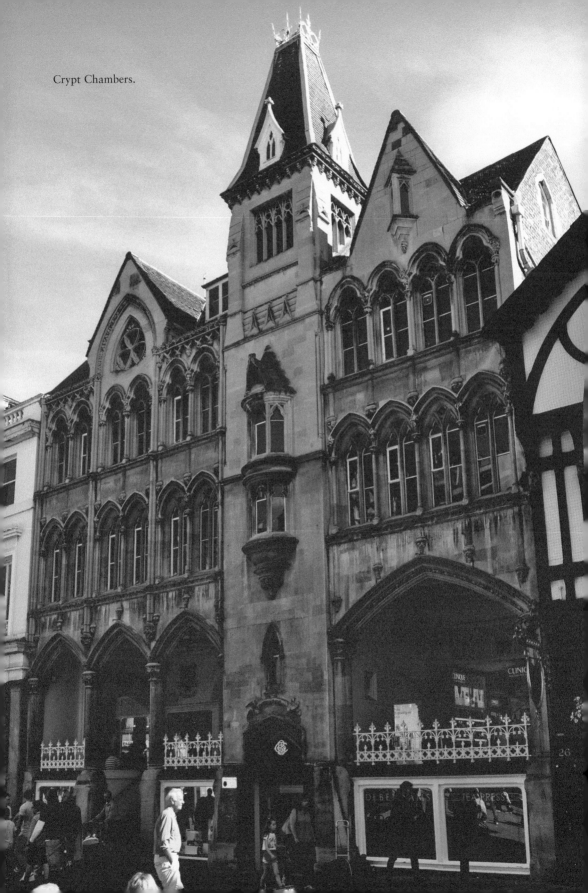

Crypt Chambers.

45. Ye Olde Boot Inn, Eastgate Street

Leaving the gate and continuing along Eastgate Street towards the High Cross we find another ancient pub, Ye Olde Boot Inn, a narrow mock-Tudor building set between two larger ones with the name on the front elevation. It first opened as an inn in 1643 and is situated on the level of the upper Row; the second storey has a bay window that extends out across the street. Although it has been refurbished over the years, most of the antiquity is still present. The cellar of the pub is below street level with a barrel vault. The walls of the barrel-vaulted stockroom are medieval, the interior is very original.

It was built in 1643 from ship's timbers taken from the boatyards in the old port of Chester and, accordingly, is one of the city's older buildings. A lot of Chester's buildings from the Stuart and Tudor period are built from the 'ribs' that came from ships in the port when they were scrapped. During the English Civil War and the Siege of Chester (1645–1646), when the pub was nice and new, it was used as a meeting place by the Royalist troops and when Cromwell's troops invaded the city they entered the Boot and shot those in there. During Victorian times the pub was used as a brothel. In those days the front of the pub was a barber's shop and a 'madam' organised the 'ladies of the night' at the rear. During the 1920s a gambling club was opened in one of the rooms.

The pub was extensively restored in the 1980s, when a time capsule from 1882 was found containing a copy of the *Cheshire Observer*. Also found during the restoration and now on display behind the bar is a small stone ball that was found embedded in one of the ancient oak beams. This is believed to be a piece of ammunition from a smoothbore gun from either the Civil War period or fired from a gun used by poachers much later. Also in the pub can be seen an area of exposed wattle and daub that make up the interior walls.

The Boot interior.

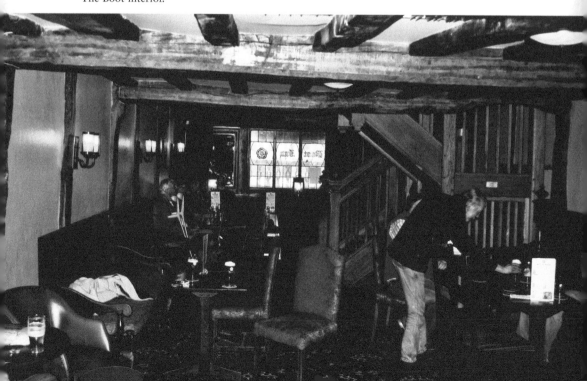

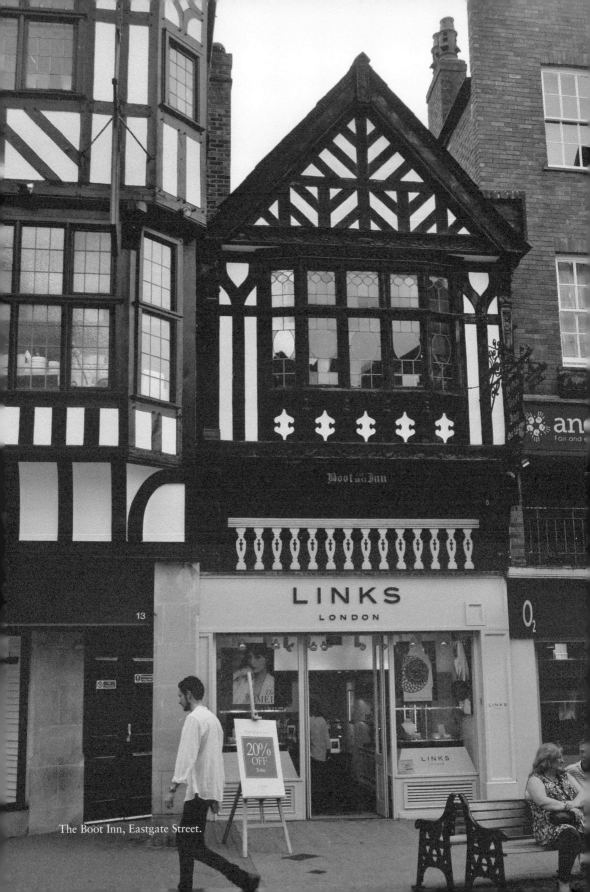

The Boot Inn, Eastgate Street.

46. The King Charles or Phoenix Tower

The Chester City Walls are one of the unique features of the city, so it would not be right to exclude at least a few examples of the buildings that are situated upon them. Joining the Walls by the Cathedral and walking anti-clockwise, the first tower that we come to is the King Charles Tower or Phoenix Tower, sometimes called the Newton Tower, which is another Grade I-listed building. The tower dates from the medieval period and by 1612, after much use, the tower's fabric was in poor condition. It was restored and above the door a plaque was affixed giving the date of 1613 and a carving of a phoenix, the emblem of the guild responsible for the restoration. During the Civil War the tower had a gun on each storey and it was damaged in the conflict. A plaque on the tower states that King Charles I stood on the tower on 24 September 1645 and watched as his soldiers were defeated at the Battle of Rowton Heath (or Rowton Moor) in the distance. The king made a temporary escape into Wales via the Old Dee Bridge.

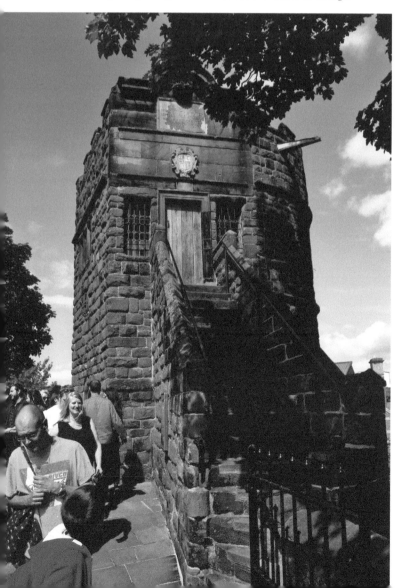

The King Charles or Phoenix Tower.

47. Morgan's Mount

Continuing along the wall we pass another Grade I-listed tower called Morgan's Mount. This was built during the Civil War as a gun and observation platform. It originally had the romantic name 'The Raised Square Platform' but this was later changed to Morgan's Mount, after a Royalist officer, Captain Edward Morgan. The gun was destroyed after the Battle of Rowton Heath in 1645.

Morgan's Mount.

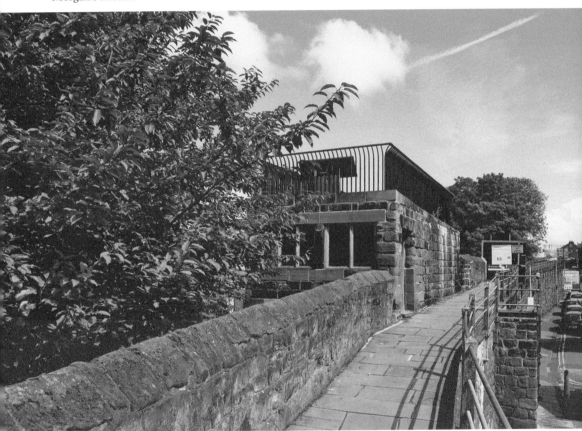

48. The Goblin Tower

We pass over the new St Martin's Gate across the Ring Road, and soon come to our next tower, known as the Goblin Tower, or Pemberton's Parlour. This unusual half tower is situated on the North Wall and was originally called Goblin Tower, a name that can still be seen at the top of it together with its rebuild date of 1894. It also bears the name Pemberton's Parlour after John Pemberton, a rope maker and Mayor of Chester in 1730. It has a well-worn sandstone tablet naming the mayors and the men responsible for repairing the wall in days gone by.

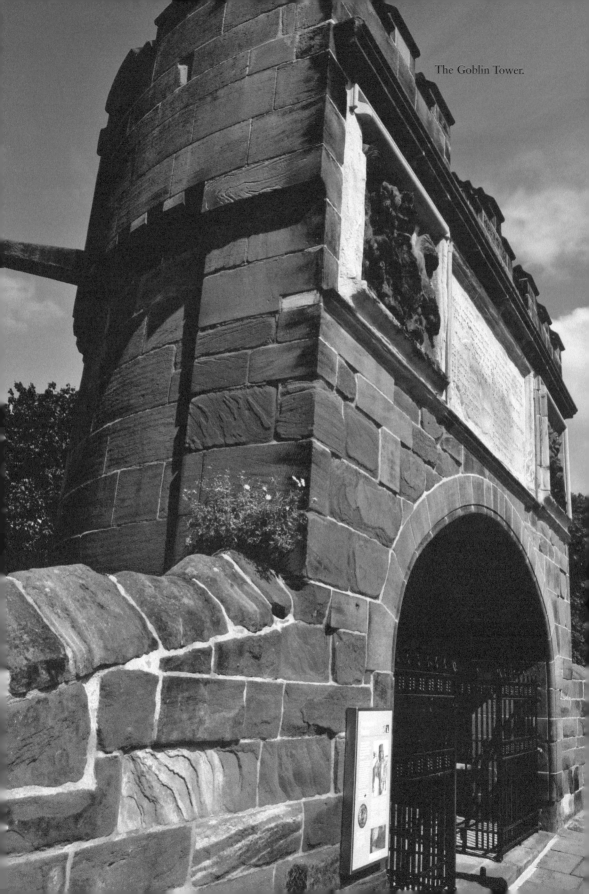

The Goblin Tower.

49. Bonewaldesthorne's Tower & Water Tower

Looking to your left is part of Chester's old port, where ships would discharge their cargo. A junction in the walls here is a spur on the left that ends with the Water Tower that was built between 1322 and 1325 and, at the time of building, stood in the River Dee.

Also here is the strangely named Bonewaldesthorne's Tower. This tower can be dated back to 1249 and it was rebuilt and altered between 1322 and 1326 to become the gatehouse to the Water Tower. In 1838 the newly formed Chester Mechanics' Institution leased the two towers from the City Council to use as a museum. The towers closed as a museum between 1901 and 1902 when the walls were rebuilt. There is, however, another attraction within, entitled 'Sick to Death: The Gory Story of Medicine Through Time'. As for the strange name – Bonewaldesthorne's – it is rumoured to be the name of an officer in the army of Aethelflaeda, the daughter of Alfred the Great who rebuilt Chester's walls in around AD 907. It could also be the name of a Chester worthy. If you look to the right, opposite Bonewaldesthorne's Tower, you will see a footpath leading down to what was the river and the Water Tower gardens: in 1849 these steps led to the privately owned Chester Baths and wash houses.

Bonewaldesthorne's Tower and the Water Tower.

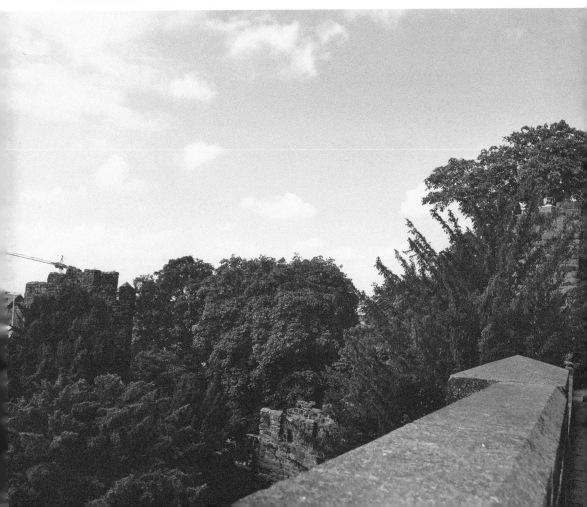

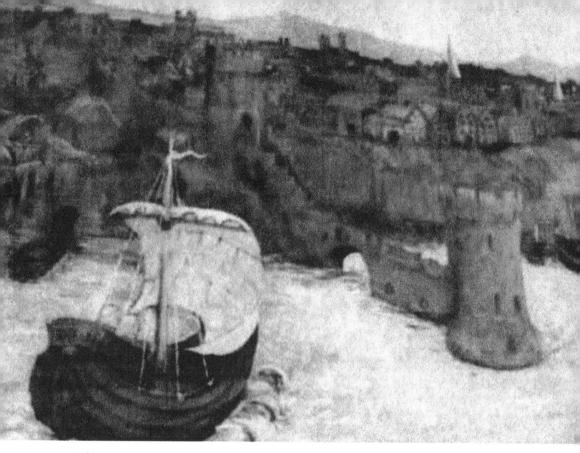

The Water Tower in medieval times.

50. Chester General Station, 2014

Chester once had two stations in the city, with others in the outlying villages. The main station was and still is Chester General station, which was a joint station and included the Holyhead Railway, the Chester and Crewe Railway and the Birkenhead Railway. These later became part of the London and North Western Railway (LNWR) and the Great Western Railway (GWR). This joint station dates from 1848. Architecturally the station has an Italianate frontage and was designed by Francis Thompson. The station also has carved wooden owls at some strategic locations high in the roof beams to help deter pigeons.

During the 1950s and prior to the Beeching cuts, Chester General was the main Chester station and the gateway to North Wales, the Irish boats from Holyhead and trains from London and throughout the country but a later station was built in 1875. This was the Chester Northgate station which was owned by the Cheshire Lines Committee (CLC). This station was the Western Terminus of the CLC line from Manchester to Chester via Northwich. The station was more convenient for local traffic than Chester General and was soon connected to Birkenhead, the Wirral and North Wales. It was given a new roof by British Railways in 1950 and in January 1960 it was closed to steam engines, after that date only Diesel Multiple Units used it. That station was demolished on 6 October 1969, all the lines were lifted and now the Northgate Arena, Chester's sports complex, occupies the site.

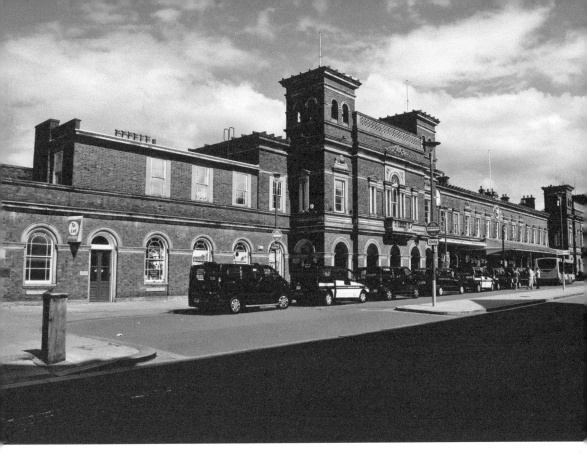

Chester General station.

About the Author

Paul Hurley is a freelance writer, author and a member of the Society of Authors. He lives in Winsford, Cheshire, with his wife Rose. He has two sons and two daughters. For more imformation please visit www.paul-hurley.co.uk.

Also by the Author

Fiction
Waffen SS Britain

Non-Fiction
Middlewich (with the late Brian Curzon)
Northwich Through Time
Winsford Through Time
Villages of Mid Cheshire Through Time
Frodsham and Helsby Through Time
Nantwich Through Time
Chester Through Time (with Len Morgan)
Middlewich & Holmes Chapel Through Time
Sandbach, Wheelock & District Through Time
Knutsford Through Time
Macclesfield Through Time
Cheshire Through Time
Northwich, Winsford & Middlewich Through Time
Chester in the 1950s
Chester in the 1960s
Villages of Mid Cheshire Through Time Revisited.
Northwich Through the Ages
Chester Pubs (with Len Morgan)
Chester History Tour
Nantwich History Tour
Macclesfield History Tour
Knutsford History Tour
Steam Nostalgia in the North of England

Acknowledgements

Thanks to my good friend Len Morgan for access to his remarkable archive of old Chester photos, to my commissioning editor, Alan Murphy for his advice and my editor Marcus Pennington for his assistance. Finally, thank you to my wife Rose for her patience during the writing and compilation of this book.

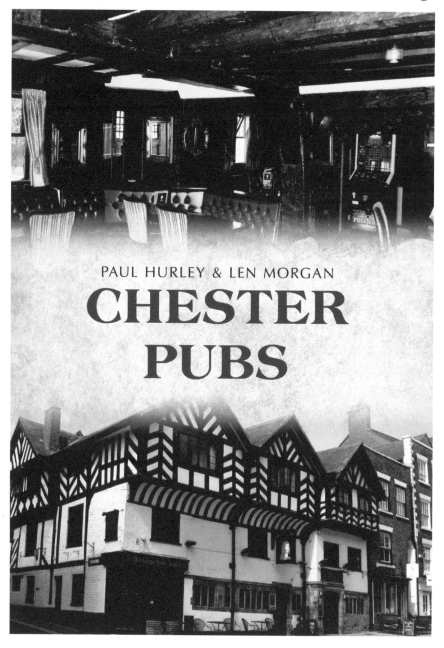